From Crash to Conflict

From Crash to Conflict

The Great Depression and the Rise of Global Extremism

By

Felix Brandt

Vij Books
New Delhi (India)

Published by

Vij Books
(Publishers, Distributors & Importers)
4836/24, 3rd Floor, Ansari Road
Delhi – 110 002
Phone: 91-11-43596460
Mobile: 98110 94883
e-mail: contact@vijpublishing.com
www.vijbooks.in

ISBN: 978-93-90349-40-1 (HB)

ISBN: 978-93-90349-64-7 (PB)

ISBN: 978-93-90349-60-9 (eBook)

This book was developed using advanced writing tools to support the drafting and ideation process. All content has been thoughtfully curated, refined, and reviewed to ensure quality and relevance.

Contents

Introduction

On a crisp autumn morning in 1929, a New York banker leaned against the marble facade of his institution and watched the crowd surge down Wall Street. Office clerks, shoe-shiners, and society women pressed shoulder to shoulder, craning their necks for news from the Stock Exchange. The ticker tape inside was stuttering—its printouts lagging minutes behind events—as prices plunged faster than machines could record. By mid-afternoon, rumours of ruined fortunes and suicides filled the air with an almost physical weight. In that instant, the world's most powerful economy revealed its fragility: prosperity, it turned out, was a brittle mask.

What began as a crash of numbers soon became a collapse of certainties. Banks shuttered their doors without warning. Factories fell silent. Families who had believed themselves secure found themselves queuing for bread alongside the destitute. Within months, the shock travelled across the Atlantic, toppling governments in Germany and Britain, crippling Japan's export industries, and sending shivers through colonial economies in Asia, Africa, and Latin America. The Depression was not a storm that passed; it was a climate that endured, reshaping the landscape of politics, society, and culture for a generation.

This book argues that the Great Depression was not merely a story of lost wealth or failed markets. It was a crucible where political extremism was forged and tempered—fascism in Europe, communism in its Soviet guise, militarism in Japan. It was not only an economic calamity but a profound psychological and cultural rupture, a breaking of trust in the very idea of liberal democracy. To trace the Depression, then, is to trace how despair can curdle into rage, how hunger can strip away the fabric of civic life, and how societies, when pressed to the edge, can abandon pluralism for the false comfort of authoritarian certainty.

A Crisis Beyond Numbers

It is tempting to read the Depression in economic shorthand: stock indices plummeting, unemployment rising, trade collapsing. Yet to do so is to mistake the skeleton for the body. Statistics measure the loss, but they cannot capture its meaning. For millions of people, the Depression was not a line on a graph but the hollow ache of an empty stomach, the humiliation of eviction, the sudden irrelevance of skills honed over decades. The factory hand in Detroit, the smallholder in Iowa, the clerk in Berlin, the miner in Wales—all found themselves united in bewilderment and defeat.

This shared vulnerability became political dynamite. When democratic governments hesitated or offered timid remedies, confidence drained away. The soup kitchen and the unemployment line became visible indictments of political failure, fuelling the rhetoric of radicals who promised swift and decisive solutions. In such moments, despair itself becomes an ideology. Hunger does not merely weaken the body; it corrodes the bonds of trust upon which democratic societies rest.

The metaphor that will run through this book is simple: the Depression was not a passing storm but an earthquake. Storms damage, but they are weathered. Earthquakes shift the ground beneath one's feet, leaving societies unsure of where stability lies. In the 1930s, that uncertainty opened cracks wide enough for extremists to march through.

The Fragile Promise of Liberal Capitalism

By the 1920s, the liberal capitalist order seemed triumphant. America had emerged from the First World War as the undisputed economic power. Germany was limping but hopeful, rebuilt with American loans. Britain still presided over an empire that stretched across the globe, and the League of Nations embodied a tentative hope for international cooperation. Yet beneath this surface lay fractures—massive debts, unstable currencies, brittle political coalitions—that the Crash would expose with brutal clarity.

The fragility of the Weimar Republic, the paralysis of Hoover's America, the dogged orthodoxy of Britain's economic policy, and the fevered industrialism of Stalin's Soviet Union all converged on a single truth: when economies fail, politics follows. The Depression made visible what had always been latent—that prosperity alone cannot guarantee stability, and that democracy is never more vulnerable than in times of mass insecurity.

The Global Reverberation

To see the Depression solely as an American tragedy is to misunderstand its reach. The Wall Street crash was a trigger, but the conditions for collapse were already embedded in a global system of debt, dependence, and fragile trade. Germany's recovery had been built on American loans; when those dried up, its political experiment unravelled. Japan, dependent on exports of silk and manufactured goods, saw its markets vanish overnight, leaving space for military leaders to claim that conquest was the only remedy. In Britain, unemployment scarred entire regions, while colonial subjects were reminded of the empire's capacity to extract but not protect.

Meanwhile, in Moscow, Soviet leaders proclaimed that communism had triumphed over capitalist chaos. Even as millions starved in Ukraine, the spectacle of apparent stability drew intellectuals from the West, who saw in the Soviet experiment a rough but appealing alternative to liberal paralysis. Ideas, no less than armies or industries, were set in motion by the Depression.

The Human Face of Collapse

The Depression etched itself not only into policy debates and party platforms but into the texture of everyday life. Photographs by Dorothea Lange, novels by Steinbeck, and the stark testimony of German diarists all reveal how people internalised the crisis. A bank run was not merely an economic event but a collective act of fear. A protest march was not simply political but existential, a way to reclaim agency in a world that seemed to have slipped beyond control.

Cultural responses matter because they show how societies make sense of catastrophe. Narratives of blame, hope, and betrayal circulate in times of crisis, shaping what people believe is possible. In the 1930s, those narratives often gravitated towards extremes: the Nazis' poisonous myth of national rebirth, the communists' promise of class redemption, the Japanese militarists' vision of imperial destiny. Ideas once confined to the margins became mainstream because they offered clarity in the fog of uncertainty.

The Book's Central Questions

This book is not content to catalogue events; it seeks to answer questions that remain urgent today. Why do some democracies survive economic catastrophe while others collapse? What makes authoritarian promises so compelling when prosperity falters? How do cultural symbols—of hunger, unemployment, and decline—become ammunition in political battles? And what lessons, if any, can we draw for an age in which financial crises, pandemics, and climate shocks again test the resilience of democratic institutions?

At stake in these questions is more than historical curiosity. The Depression teaches us that economic collapse is never confined to balance sheets. It penetrates into identity, community, and imagination. It rearranges what societies believe about fairness, authority, and the future. If we listen closely, the voices of the 1930s still echo in our own anxieties.

A Warning Across Time

The final years of the Depression did not end in recovery but in war. Germany's economic despair translated into Hitler's expansionism; Japan's collapse underpinned its drive for empire; the failure of international cooperation left the world defenceless against aggression. By 1939, the earthquake of 1929 had produced a geopolitical eruption.

This book does not suggest that history repeats in tidy cycles. But it insists that the dynamics of collapse—fear, mistrust, the search for certainty—remain constants of human societies. The Great Depression stands as both a historical moment and a mirror. To study it is to confront not only the fragility of the past but the vulnerabilities of our present.

An Invitation

What follows is not a narrow economic chronicle but a journey through the lived, political, and cultural dimensions of collapse. It moves from the stock market's implosion to the breadlines of Chicago, from the fractured parliaments of Berlin and Tokyo to the uneasy calm of British coal towns, from Soviet propaganda posters to the photographs of dust-blown migrants on American highways.

The aim is not merely to recount but to reveal: how economic fragility undermines democracy, how despair paves the road to extremism, and how the choices societies make in times of crisis determine whether they emerge reformed or ruined.

The Depression remains our warning that when the ground beneath us shifts, the direction we choose—towards solidarity or division, reform or repression—defines not only recovery but destiny. This book invites readers to stand at that crossroads once more, to understand how the 1930s set the world aflame, and to ask, with fresh urgency, what lessons we dare ignore today.

Chapter 1

When the Market Fell Silent

On the morning of Thursday, 24 October 1929, the trading floor of the New York Stock Exchange resembled less a marketplace than a theatre of panic. A thousand brokers shouted themselves hoarse as the tickers lagged, their spools spitting out fragments of a story already galloping ahead of them. Prices were collapsing too quickly to follow. Secretaries sprinted through corridors with frantic notes, while messengers darted between offices with orders already outdated by the time they arrived. Outside, the crowd swelled. Clerks, delivery boys, and society matrons gathered in the street, drawn by the irresistible spectacle of the financial world's implosion. What they saw was not merely the unraveling of fortunes, but the unmasking of an illusion. Prosperity, they realised, had been nothing more than confidence dressed as certainty. And confidence, once broken, dissolves with frightening speed.

This sudden rupture confounded a nation that had been assured of endless growth. The 1920s had been celebrated as a decade of triumph—of motorcars and radios, of skyscrapers and jazz, of stock tickers that seemed to climb forever. Newspapers hailed the market as a democratic engine of wealth, a place where the clerk could, in theory, stand shoulder to shoulder with the tycoon. Economists and columnists assured readers that science had tamed volatility, that prosperity had found permanence. But when the crash came, it exposed the fragility of a system built on faith. The first casualty was not capital but conviction—the belief that the future could be relied upon.

What followed was less a rational recalibration than a collective unravelling. Investors, large and small, did not calmly assess their positions. They fled. Panic selling spread through the exchanges as if fear were contagious, and indeed it was. Loss was magnified by imagination: each falling share price seemed a prelude to total ruin. The behaviour resembled not reasoned calculation but stampede, the same psychology that drives a crowd to crush itself in its rush for a single exit. The historian who lingers too long over balance sheets risks missing the deeper truth: that collapses of this scale are human dramas, propelled as much by emotion as by arithmetic.

The crack of Wall Street's foundations reverberated across oceans. In London, where Britain already staggered under the weight of debt and industrial decline, the tremor deepened doubts about the empire's durability. In Germany, whose fragile recovery rested on American loans, the withdrawal of credit proved devastating. What had been a precarious democracy suddenly found itself without economic oxygen, and extremism thrived in the vacuum. In Japan, where silk exports underpinned the economy, the collapse of demand destroyed livelihoods overnight, sharpening the appeal of those who claimed that conquest abroad was the only escape. The Depression was not a parochial misfortune; it was a global rupture, demonstrating how intimately the fates of nations had become bound together.

For ordinary citizens, the abstractions of finance translated into stark, unforgettable images: the silent factory floor, the soup kitchen queue, the eviction notice nailed to a front door. These were not just symptoms of economic decline; they were symbols of betrayal, proof that the promises of modernity had been false. A father pacing outside a closed bank, children watching their belongings piled on the kerb—such scenes resonated far beyond individual households. They carried an emotional charge that politicians could not ignore and demagogues would later exploit. Economic pain, when made visible, acquires political power.

The deeper wound, however, lay in the erosion of trust. Citizens who had once believed in the competence of governments and the wisdom of institutions began to doubt both. If leaders could not protect savings, jobs, or homes, what legitimacy did they deserve? This question, whispered at first, grew louder as months turned into years. The loss of faith proved more corrosive than any financial contraction, for it gnawed at the very glue that binds democratic societies together: the conviction that shared institutions are capable of managing shared crises.

This chapter traces the transformation of October 1929 from a market collapse into a political earthquake. It begins with the drama of the crash itself, where prosperity's mask slipped in a matter of days. It then delves into the psychology of panic, revealing how fear spreads more swiftly than reason and why personal despair can metastasise into national destabilisation. The lens then widens to show how this implosion travelled across borders, destabilising economies already poised on the edge. Along the way, we will linger on the potent symbols of collapse—images that condensed economic despair into cultural shorthand—and we will examine how these early shocks seeded a broader distrust in democratic leadership.

What lies ahead is not a tale of numbers but of meanings: how societies experience collapse, how they interpret it, and how those interpretations shape the paths they choose. The silence that fell after the roar of the markets was not empty; it was filled with the murmurs of doubt, the whispers of blame, and the tentative first words of extremism. To understand that silence is to understand why the Depression became not only an economic event but the opening act of a decade that would end in global war.

And so, we begin where confidence ended—on the trading floor of October 1929, when the clamour of prosperity gave way to a silence more ominous than any noise. The silence of markets stilled, of factories closed, of voices unsure of what to believe. The silence before the world's political foundations began to crack.

The Crash That Shook Confidence

On 23 October 1929, the mood on Wall Street was still buoyant enough for brokers to imagine that the storm clouds gathering over the market might soon disperse. The previous years had offered intoxicating proof of modern finance's promise: a stock exchange that appeared to rise without gravity, credit available to anyone willing to seize it, and a culture convinced that prosperity was not merely cyclical but permanent. By the next day, however, the illusion collapsed. "Black Thursday" entered the lexicon as investors, desperate to liquidate, flooded the market with sell orders. By the closing bell, billions of dollars in paper wealth had vanished. That spectacle—the ticker tapes failing to keep pace, the police called in to restrain panicked crowds outside the Exchange—became the first act in a drama that would unravel the confidence of an entire civilisation.

The shock was not simply the loss of capital but the revelation of fragility. Finance had been dressed up as science, a domain of charts, ratios, and rational calculation, yet its foundations rested on something far less tangible: belief. As long as people trusted in the system, credit flowed, shares rose, and prosperity seemed secure. Once doubt set in, the edifice crumbled with astonishing speed. The stock market's collapse exposed a paradox at the heart of modern capitalism: the stronger the faith in endless growth, the more devastating the rupture when that faith failed.

Behind the drama of falling share prices lay the more corrosive damage to psychology. Middle-class savers who had been told that the market was a safe ladder to wealth saw their savings annihilated. Banks that had extended easy credit were suddenly unable to collect, and rumours of insolvency sparked queues of anxious depositors demanding their money. Confidence, once eroded, did not decline gradually; it collapsed. People withdrew from markets, from banks, even from spending itself, hoarding what little they had. The shock of October 1929 was therefore not a mere downturn in value but a collective trauma—a reminder that the security of modern finance was always contingent, never guaranteed.

The imagery of the crash was unforgettable. Men who had strutted with paper profits days before now sat slumped on kerbstones, faces pale, ties loosened, staring at numbers that no longer meant anything. Newspapers, groping for language, spoke of panic, hysteria, contagion. It was as though the rational world of contracts and dividends had given way to something primal: a stampede. That stampede was not confined to Wall Street. Across the United States, small investors liquidated holdings, businesses cut payrolls in anticipation of leaner days, and banks, frightened of collapse, withdrew credit. The shock rippled outward in widening circles.

What made the crisis so destabilising was the speed with which private despair translated into public fragility. A single family losing its savings was a tragedy; thousands doing so simultaneously became a political problem. The legitimacy of institutions depends not only on their laws and offices but on the confidence of citizens that those institutions are competent. In 1929, that confidence evaporated almost overnight. Ordinary Americans, who had been encouraged to see the stock market as a gateway to democratic prosperity, now faced eviction and unemployment. Disillusionment, once seeded, did not remain private; it reshaped the collective mood of a nation.

The collapse also revealed the deep interdependence of the modern financial order. Germany, still crippled by reparations from the First World War, had been living on American loans. When Wall Street faltered, those loans dried up, and the fragile Weimar Republic began to suffocate. In Britain, struggling with declining industries and a heavy debt burden, the crash intensified pressure on the pound sterling and fuelled doubts about the empire's economic durability. In Japan, reliant on silk exports, the collapse of global demand devastated rural communities and set the stage for political upheaval. Thus, what began in Manhattan was not contained; it was globalised almost instantly, demonstrating that the architecture of interwar capitalism was far more fragile than its architects had admitted.

At the heart of this fragility was a contradiction. Modern finance promised stability through innovation: new instruments, new credit mechanisms, new institutions. Yet those very innovations increased exposure to volatility. Buying shares "on margin"—with borrowed money—multiplied both gains and losses. Banks that had blurred the line between deposit-taking and speculation found themselves vulnerable to shocks. The same networks that had knitted the world together after 1918—trade flows, credit arrangements, gold-standard commitments—now transmitted weakness as efficiently as they had once transmitted growth.

The crash was thus not a freak accident but a revelation of how brittle the system had always been. And it was more than a revelation of economics: it was a rupture in the cultural faith of the West. The Enlightenment promise that reason and progress would deliver security met its limits on the floor of the Exchange. In its place came uncertainty, anxiety, and a search for new answers. That search would lead some toward reform and resilience, but many more toward the dangerous allure of extremism.

Symbols of the collapse carried a potency numbers could not. The soup kitchen line, stretching for blocks in cities once brimming with confidence; the shuttered factory gates that had provided generations with stability; the hollowed faces of children in photographs circulated worldwide—these became emblems of broken promises. Such imagery did not merely record economic pain; it redefined it, turning abstract failure into visceral proof of betrayal. Political actors seized upon these symbols, weaving them into narratives of blame and redemption. For radicals, the crash was a godsend, a ready-made argument that the old order was beyond saving.

Trust in leaders faltered alongside trust in markets. When governments hesitated, clung to orthodoxy, or failed to stem the tide, citizens began to doubt their competence. In Germany, each banking crisis further undermined Weimar democracy. In America, President Hoover's insistence that recovery was just around the corner struck many as delusion. In Britain, the formation of a national government revealed elites' desperation to preserve stability at any cost, even if innovation was sacrificed. In each case, the erosion of political confidence proved at least as damaging as the economic downturn itself.

The collapse of October 1929 therefore deserves to be understood not merely as a financial disaster but as the first psychological blow to global capitalism. It punctured the illusion that modernity had conquered instability and exposed the unsettling truth that prosperity rested on the shifting sands of belief. The silence that followed—the hushed trading floors, the shuttered banks, the mute disbelief of ruined investors—was more eloquent than any headline. It was the silence of confidence extinguished.

Yet silence is never permanent. Into the void rushed competing voices: some calling for reform, others for revolution, and still others for vengeance. The crash created not just a financial vacuum but a political one, and vacuums do not remain empty for long. The years that followed would demonstrate how quickly despair could harden into ideology, and how the collapse of markets could presage the collapse of democracies.

The crash that shook confidence, then, was more than a moment of panic; it was the beginning of a decade in which the foundations of liberal society itself were tested. The question it raised—what happens when belief in the future disintegrates?—remains as unsettling today as it was in 1929. And it is to that question, and its reverberations across nations, that we now turn.

Panic and the Psychology of Loss

The collapse of October 1929 was not, at its core, a story of mathematics. Balance sheets mattered, yes, but what turned a stock market correction into a global cataclysm was not arithmetic but emotion. The paradox of modern finance is that it depends on rational calculation while being perpetually vulnerable to irrational stampedes. Investors know, in theory, that panic selling destroys value, yet in practice they rush to the exits in unison, each driven by the fear of being the last left inside. The market functions on numbers but lives on trust, and when trust fractures, fear fills the void.

Accounts from the trading floor make this truth painfully vivid. Brokers shouted contradictory orders, the ticker tape lagged hopelessly behind events, and rumours coursed through the crowd faster than facts could be verified. Those who had, only days before, assured their clients that prosperity was eternal now urged them to sell at any price. The spectacle was not one of deliberation but of contagion—behaviour more reminiscent of a crowd fleeing a fire than of investors calmly adjusting their portfolios. What burned was not only money but certainty, and in its place rose the intoxicating, paralysing force of collective fear.

Psychologists have long observed that losses loom larger than gains. Daniel Kahneman and Amos Tversky, decades after the Depression, would codify this into "loss aversion": the principle that people will go to extraordinary lengths to avoid losses greater than they would to achieve equivalent gains.

The market panic of 1929 was an empirical demonstration before the theory had a name. Investors, terrified of losing more, sold in waves even when rational analysis suggested patience. The urge was not to optimise but to survive. In such moments, the individual's calculation is inseparable from the crowd's. Seeing neighbours ruin themselves instils not caution but imitation. Fear, once visible, multiplies.

The contagion was not limited to those who held stocks. Bank runs, which became a defining feature of the Depression, revealed how psychology could unravel institutions that were technically solvent. A single whisper—*this bank may not have enough reserves*—was enough to produce a queue outside its doors. Each depositor, acting rationally in isolation, sought to withdraw funds before collapse. Collectively, their actions created the very collapse they feared. Thus, what began as anxiety became prophecy, fulfilled by the crowd itself. Confidence is a strange commodity: it exists only insofar as people believe in it, and once disbelief spreads, it evaporates entirely.

The consequences of this psychological unravelling reached far beyond finance. For a factory worker in Detroit or a miner in the Ruhr, the panic of bankers might have seemed distant. Yet as firms lost credit, production slowed, and unemployment rose, the fear at the top cascaded downward. Personal despair—an empty wallet, an eviction notice, the inability to provide for a family—was born of collective panic. And once despair became widespread, it destabilised not just markets but the legitimacy of governments. People began to ask whether their leaders could be trusted to protect them, and in that question lay the seed of political radicalism.

It is important to recognise that fear does not simply distort decision-making; it reshapes identity. In the Depression, the unemployed did not think of themselves merely as workers temporarily without wages. Many felt stripped of dignity, excluded from the social order, invisible or unwanted. Despair of this kind corrodes the bonds of citizenship. A population that sees itself as abandoned is far more likely to turn to those who promise belonging, however harsh the terms. The psychology of loss thus bridges the gap between the trading floor and the political rally. The emotional logic that drives a man to sell his shares in panic is not entirely separate from the one that drives him to listen to a demagogue's call for order and revenge.

The wildfire nature of panic also reveals a deeper philosophical problem: the fragility of reason in collective life. Modern societies flatter themselves with the language of rational choice, efficient markets, and enlightened governance. Yet moments of crisis expose how thin that veneer can be. When fear seizes the crowd, the calculations of the few are swept away. Even those who understand the irrationality of panic often succumb to it, unwilling to stand against the tide. In 1929, seasoned bankers liquidated alongside amateurs, not because they believed it wise, but because no one wanted to be the last clinging to a sinking ship.

One of the most haunting aspects of the Depression is how quickly fear became normalised. Within months, newspaper readers grew accustomed to headlines of failing banks, collapsing firms, and spiralling unemployment. What would once have been considered exceptional misfortune came to feel inevitable. This normalisation deepened the crisis by dulling the will to resist it. People who no longer believed recovery was possible were less likely to invest, spend, or even seek work, reinforcing the cycle of decline. The psychological spiral was not an aberration but a central mechanism of the Depression itself.

Nor is this dynamic confined to the 1930s. The global financial crisis of 2008 offered a sobering reminder of how quickly panic can return, even in an age of advanced modelling and sophisticated central banking. Markets froze not because the world's assets had suddenly lost value but because participants no longer trusted each other. Fear, once again, proved more powerful than data. The enduring lesson is that economies are not machines but human systems, and humans, when threatened, often privilege instinct over reason.

The panic of 1929 demonstrates a truth as old as civilisation: trust is the most valuable asset any society possesses, and it is also the most fragile. Lose it, and numbers on paper become meaningless; restore it, and recovery becomes possible. The Depression reminds us that confidence cannot be decreed by governments or conjured by economists. It must be believed.

Yet here lies the tension that carries us forward. If collective fear can dismantle democracies as swiftly as it dismantles markets, what, if anything, can contain it? Can institutions ever be robust enough to withstand the psychology of loss? Or is the fragility of confidence an enduring vulnerability, one that ensures each generation will face its own moment of reckoning when fear once more overwhelms reason? The silence that followed the panic of 1929 left those questions suspended, waiting for history to answer.

The Global Shockwave

On the morning after Black Thursday, most Americans saw the stock market collapse as a national tragedy. Few yet grasped that the tremors radiating outward from Wall Street would soon topple the fragile architecture of global finance. Yet within weeks, London bankers felt the chill of vanished credit, German factories slowed for lack of capital, and Japanese farmers watched the price of silk—their lifeblood export—plummet by half. The crisis did not respect borders. What began as an American implosion revealed how deeply entangled the world's economies had become, and how vulnerable nations were to shocks beyond their control.

The paradox was stark: the 1920s had promised prosperity through interdependence. The world had tied itself together with new financial cords—loans, reparations, trade flows—believing that connection would bring stability. Instead, when the United States faltered, the cords became conduits for collapse. Far from insulating one another, economies dragged each other down. The crash showed that modern capitalism's greatest strength—its global reach—was also its deepest weakness.

Britain was the first to feel the reverberation. Still recovering from the fiscal strains of the First World War, it carried enormous debts and clung stubbornly to the gold standard. Wall Street's crisis tightened credit across the Atlantic, making it more expensive for London to financc its obligations. Export industries in the north—coal, steel, textiles—were already declining, and the contraction in global trade pushed unemployment above two million by 1930. The financial pressure culminated in the 1931 sterling crisis, when Britain was forced to abandon the gold standard altogether. The empire that had once underwritten global finance now signalled its own fragility. For many, this was more than an economic humiliation; it was a symbolic admission that the old imperial order was no longer the guarantor of stability.

Germany's predicament was more acute still. The Weimar Republic had survived the hyperinflation of 1923 by binding itself to American loans through the Dawes Plan and later the Young Plan. These loans fuelled industrial recovery and financed reparations payments to France and Britain. When Wall Street collapsed, the flow of capital ceased. American banks called in debts, and German firms, unable to refinance, collapsed in succession. By 1932, six million Germans were unemployed, and despair permeated every corner of society. The Depression was not the origin of Germany's political extremism, but it was its accelerant. Without the crash,

Hitler might have remained a fringe agitator. With it, he found an audience ready to listen to his blend of rage, scapegoating, and promises of rebirth.

Japan's crisis came through its reliance on exports. The nation's farmers depended on silk, which accounted for nearly half of foreign trade. When American and European consumers cut spending, silk prices collapsed by as much as 60 per cent. Rural communities descended into poverty almost overnight. Families sold daughters into servitude, malnutrition spread, and discontent surged. In this climate, civilian politicians lost credibility, while military leaders gained ground with the argument that Japan's salvation lay not in free trade but in territorial expansion. The invasion of Manchuria in 1931 was not an isolated act of aggression; it was an economic strategy born of despair. Japan's turn toward empire was inseparable from the Depression's destruction of export markets.

The shockwaves reached beyond these major powers. In Latin America, nations like Brazil and Argentina, dependent on coffee and beef exports, saw demand collapse, forcing political elites to rethink their reliance on foreign markets. Some responded with authoritarian regimes and protectionist policies, while others experimented with industrialisation. In colonial Asia and Africa, falling commodity prices deepened resentment toward imperial powers, who often imposed austerity to protect metropolitan interests. Thus, the Depression was not merely a Western drama; it was a catalyst for discontent in territories long subordinated to European economies.

At the heart of this global cascade was the rigidity of the gold standard. Nations remained tethered to it in the hope that stability would reassure investors. Instead, it trapped governments in policies of deflation and austerity. Central banks raised interest rates to defend currencies, further contracting their economies. Britain's abandonment of the gold standard in 1931 demonstrated both the futility of orthodoxy and the willingness of nations to prioritise survival over international cooperation. Once the linchpin of the global system was broken, a wave of competitive devaluations and trade barriers followed, fragmenting the world economy into rival blocs.

The crisis also exposed the impotence of international institutions. The League of Nations, already fragile, lacked the authority to coordinate economic responses. Conferences were convened, agreements drafted, but the political will to sacrifice national interest for collective stability was absent. Each nation turned inward, and in doing so deepened the collective spiral. The global order that had been tentatively constructed after 1918 collapsed under the weight of national protectionism.

The Depression therefore cannot be understood as a series of parallel national crises; it was a single, interconnected event. The fate of a miner in Wales, a clerk in Berlin, or a silk farmer in Nagano was linked, however invisibly, to the collapse of Wall Street credit. Globalisation, hailed in the 1920s as a guarantee of prosperity, revealed its darker side in the 1930s: vulnerability without recourse. The very interdependence that had promised stability ensured that collapse, when it came, was shared.

This interconnection carries a sobering lesson. Economic integration does not necessarily prevent catastrophe; it can accelerate and magnify it. Trust in the system was not enough to shield societies when the system itself proved brittle. The Great Depression taught the world that prosperity built on credit and fragile cooperation can unravel in an instant, leaving nations to face not only financial ruin but political upheaval.

Yet the deeper question remains unsettled. If interdependence spreads collapse as efficiently as growth, can any global order be made truly resilient? Or does every age of prosperity carry within it the seeds of a shock that will one day radiate outward, shaking societies far beyond its point of origin? The global shockwave of 1929 left that question unanswered, its reverberations still felt in the uncertainties of our own time.

Symbols of Collapse

In 1931, a photographer captured a stark image on the streets of Chicago: hundreds of men, caps pulled low against the cold, stood in a queue that wound around the block. Above them, in mocking contrast, a billboard proclaimed *"World's Highest Standard of Living – There's No Way Like the American Way"*, its painted image of a smiling white family driving a gleaming car through rolling green countryside. The juxtaposition was unmissable. On the ground, hunger and humiliation; on the billboard, the fantasy of endless prosperity. That dissonance between lived experience and promised abundance became one of the enduring symbols of the Great Depression. It was not simply that people suffered, but that their suffering stood in direct contradiction to the narratives of modernity and progress they had been told to believe.

Symbols mattered because they distilled complex economic forces into images ordinary people could grasp and feel. A shuttered factory did more than signal declining output: it embodied abandonment. Families walking past idle machines or silent assembly lines were not calculating GDP contractions; they were absorbing the message that their labour, once indispensable, was now expendable. The sight of rusting gates and weeds reclaiming factory yards became shorthand for a betrayal—proof that the social contract between industry, labour, and government had been broken.

The soup kitchen line carried an equally heavy charge. In the United States, long queues outside churches or hastily organised charity halls turned hunger into a public spectacle. For men raised to see work as the measure of dignity, accepting a ladle of soup in full view of neighbours was more than economic deprivation; it was social shame. Politically, these queues provided demagogues and reformers alike with visual evidence of system failure. In speeches and pamphlets, photographs of breadlines became weapons, proof that capitalism had not only stumbled but collapsed in plain sight.

Across the Atlantic, other symbols took root. In Britain, the hunger marches that set out from distressed industrial towns, their banners reading "Work or Full Maintenance," provided images of collective desperation. Columns of unemployed men tramping through the rain were impossible to ignore. They brought economic suffering out of private homes and into the public square, forcing parliament and press alike to confront what statistics alone could never convey. The marches dramatised inequality: in London, affluent shoppers walked past exhausted men who had crossed the country on foot simply to demand bread and dignity.

In Germany, the sight of families huddled outside shuttered banks became a potent reminder of the nation's vulnerability. People remembered vividly the hyperinflation of 1923, when life savings had dissolved into worthlessness overnight. Now, a decade later, they faced the opposite horror: deflation, unemployment, and credit collapse. Photographs of children playing with worthless banknotes from the earlier crisis often circulated alongside new images of unemployment queues, reinforcing the sense that democracy had delivered only cycles of humiliation. For extremist parties, these images were invaluable. They allowed Hitler and his followers to present themselves not merely as political actors but as interpreters of shared pain, offering easy scapegoats in place of complex causes.

In Japan, the symbols were more rural than urban. The collapse of silk exports devastated peasant families. Scenes of daughters sold into servitude, often euphemistically described as "adoptions," spread through newspapers and gossip alike. These tragedies crystallised the economic pain into moral outrage. The civilian government's impotence in preventing such degradation became a rallying cry for militarists, who insisted that territorial expansion was the only path to restore dignity and stability. Here again, the image of suffering became political currency.

The Depression also produced its own cultural record of collapse. Photographers like Dorothea Lange and Walker Evans, commissioned in the United States to document rural poverty, created images that transcended reportage. Lange's portrait of a weathered Californian mother, eyes cast to the horizon as her children cling to her shoulders, became an icon of endurance under despair. Such images did not merely reflect reality; they shaped it, influencing public opinion and policy by giving the crisis a human face. They made suffering impossible to abstract or ignore.

Symbols of collapse acquire their power precisely because they are visible and repeatable. A statistic might impress economists, but a breadline impresses everyone. Images flatten complexity, turning structural failure into a shared, almost visceral recognition of decline. They become ammunition in political discourse because they bypass argument and go straight to emotion. A politician could recite figures of unemployment; showing a queue outside a relief station accomplished more in an instant.

Yet the power of symbols cuts both ways. For some, they inspired solidarity. Neighbours organised relief, churches opened their doors, trade unions rallied members. For others, they provoked resentment and blame, sharpening divisions along class, ethnic, or ideological lines. A shuttered factory could be read as evidence of capitalist failure, communist sabotage, foreign competition, or government incompetence, depending on the storyteller. What mattered was not only the image itself but the narrative attached to it.

This raises a deeper question about human societies: why do we need images to grasp truths we already know? People were aware of unemployment, hunger, and eviction through their own experiences. Yet the sight of others in the same condition gave those experiences collective meaning. Symbols transform private despair into public reality. They provide proof that suffering is not isolated but systemic, and in doing so, they create the emotional ground on which political movements can build.

The Great Depression demonstrated that crises are fought not only in parliaments and banks but in the theatre of perception. Whoever controlled the imagery of collapse could claim authority over its interpretation. Was the soup kitchen line evidence of failed government, or of individual weakness? Was the abandoned factory proof that capitalism had exhausted itself, or that enemies within had sabotaged prosperity? Competing movements answered differently, but all recognised the central fact: the politics of the 1930s would be waged as much through symbols as through speeches.

The enduring relevance of these images reminds us that societies do not respond to crises in purely rational ways. We remember not the percentage of trade lost or the precise unemployment figure of 1932, but the breadline, the shuttered mine, the mother clutching her children in a migrant camp. These images endure because they crystallise complexity into forms the human mind can hold and pass on. They also warn us that perception is as consequential as fact. In times of collapse, what people see often matters more than what they know.

The unanswered tension is this: when the next crisis comes, which images will define it? In a world saturated by media, will symbols of collapse carry the same power, or will their ubiquity dull their effect? The lesson of the 1930s is that photographs and spectacles did not merely document history; they shaped it. Whether future societies will be moved to solidarity or to division by the images of their own crises remains the most pressing question.

Seeds of Distrust

In 1930, an American journalist described visiting a Midwestern town where the bank had closed its doors without warning. Families gathered in the street, clutching passbooks that now amounted to nothing. Their anger was not only at the bankers who had gambled recklessly, but at the officials in Washington who seemed powerless to intervene. "They have left us with nothing but words," one man spat, shaking a crumpled statement from his congressman. The fury was not unique to that town; it captured a sentiment that was spreading across continents. When prosperity evaporated, so too did faith in those entrusted to safeguard it.

The Great Depression was as much a political crisis as an economic one, because the collapse of confidence extended beyond markets to the very institutions of democracy. Citizens had been told that representative governments, guided by reason and law, could steer them through adversity. Yet when the test came, many leaders clung to orthodoxy, hesitated, or offered remedies so meagre that they seemed insulting. This failure planted seeds of distrust that would prove more dangerous than the initial financial collapse. Economies could recover with time, but once legitimacy withered, the social fabric itself began to fray.

Nowhere was this clearer than in Weimar Germany. Scarred by the memory of hyperinflation in 1923, German policymakers refused expansive stimulus when unemployment surged after 1929. Instead, Chancellor Heinrich Brüning pursued austerity: cutting spending, raising taxes, and insisting on reparations payments. For ordinary Germans, this felt like cruelty disguised as prudence. The queues for bread lengthened, but the government's speeches extolled discipline. Trust drained away not gradually but in torrents. In election after election, the centre crumbled while extremists—Nazis and communists alike—offered certainty. The collapse of faith in moderate leadership was not a side-effect of the Depression; it was the mechanism through which democracy itself unravelled.

The United States faced a different, but related, dilemma. President Herbert Hoover was an able administrator and a man of genuine compassion, yet his philosophy of self-reliance paralysed him. He insisted that the downturn was temporary, that voluntary cooperation and minimal government aid would suffice. Each reassurance rang hollow as unemployment climbed. For millions, Hoover became a symbol not of stability but of denial. Shantytowns of the destitute were derisively nicknamed "Hoovervilles." The ridicule revealed something deeper: the president had lost not merely authority but credibility. It was Franklin Roosevelt's great political talent to recognise that trust could be restored only by visible action and by rhetoric that acknowledged people's fear.

Britain, too, struggled to sustain confidence in democratic governance. Faced with spiralling deficits and mounting unemployment, leaders formed the National Government in 1931, a coalition meant to preserve stability. Yet its reliance on spending cuts and its failure to revive depressed regions left many disillusioned. Hunger marches, like the famous Jarrow Crusade of 1936, showed how far citizens had lost faith in London's willingness—or ability—to respond. The fact that Britain's democracy ultimately survived did not erase the scars of mistrust that lingered in industrial communities for decades.

The common thread across nations was that citizens looked to democratic institutions for protection and found hesitation, orthodoxy, or denial. In each case, the gap between expectation and performance widened into disillusionment. Trust is a peculiar kind of political currency: hard to earn, easy to squander, and almost impossible to conjure in a crisis once lost.

The Depression revealed that governments are judged less on the scale of their resources than on the clarity of their actions. A small but decisive intervention can inspire confidence; a large but delayed one can destroy it.

The philosophical lesson runs deeper still. Democracies depend not only on ballots and constitutions but on a cultural glue: the belief that leaders act in good faith, that institutions, though imperfect, can manage common crises. When that belief weakens, democracy becomes vulnerable to challengers who promise certainty. Extremists thrive not because they offer better solutions—rarely do they even attempt them—but because they feed on distrust. Hitler's rise was inseparable from the conviction, shared by millions, that Weimar politicians were incapable of decisive action. The same was true in Japan, where civilian governments appeared powerless against economic collapse, clearing the way for military leaders who claimed to embody resolve.

This connection between distrust and extremism gives the Depression its enduring relevance. Economic hardship alone does not topple democracies. Britain endured mass unemployment, the United States endured bank failures, and both ultimately survived. What distinguished cases like Germany was the erosion of trust to the point where democracy itself lost legitimacy. When people ceased to believe that the system could respond to their needs, they turned to alternatives that promised to bypass compromise, procedure, and pluralism altogether.

Symbols of collapse—breadlines, shuttered factories, homeless families—became political ammunition precisely because they confirmed the sense that leaders were failing. Every soup kitchen photograph was a critique of government, every hunger march a rebuke of parliamentary inaction. The images resonated not only because of the suffering they depicted but because of the void they implied: if this is happening, where is our leadership? Extremists needed no elaborate argument; the symbols themselves did the work.

It is tempting to imagine that trust, once lost, can be rebuilt by growth alone. Yet history suggests otherwise. Economic recovery may restore jobs and output, but political legitimacy requires more: acknowledgement of failure, visible reform, and a willingness to adapt institutions to new realities. Roosevelt's fireside chats, for example, were less about technical policy than about restoring the emotional bond between citizen and state. He understood that trust is not abstract but personal, rooted in whether people believe that their leaders *see* them.

The Depression thus leaves us with an unsettling truth: the gravest danger in a crisis is not the initial shock but the corrosion of trust that follows. Democracies survive on confidence that they are capable of self-correction. Once that confidence is gone, the path is open for those who insist that only authoritarian certainty can deliver stability.

And so a question lingers. When the next great crisis comes—and it will—will democratic leaders act swiftly and decisively enough to preserve trust? Or will hesitation and denial once again plant seeds of distrust that grow into something far more destructive than the collapse of markets? The 1930s suggest that the answer may determine not only economic recovery but the very survival of democracy itself.

Chapter 2

Breadlines and Barricades

In the winter of 1932, men in threadbare coats lined the pavements of New York, waiting for a ladle of broth or a crust of bread. The queues snaked for blocks, silent but eloquent, a daily indictment of the government that claimed to represent them. Hunger, once a private shame, had become a public spectacle. Newspapers carried photographs of respectable clerks and labourers reduced to beggars, and the effect was electric. A citizenry that had been told to trust in markets and self-reliance now stood in full view of one another, evidence that both promises had failed. Food queues became more than relief: they were symbols of broken legitimacy, reminders that hunger was not merely an individual hardship but a collective political condition.

For millions, the collapse of work proved even more corrosive than the collapse of wages. A job was not just income—it was identity, rhythm, and recognition. When factories closed and offices shed staff, people lost more than livelihoods; they lost their place in the social order. A man without work was, in his own eyes and in those of his community, diminished. Families strained under the weight of shame, marriages faltered, and the young learned quickly that opportunity was a mirage. This vacuum of belonging created fertile ground for ideologues who promised solidarity, dignity, and a role in a grander project—whether the nation, the class, or the race.

The streets soon became stages where private despair turned public. Protests began with bread-and-butter demands—higher relief payments, shorter hours, jobs for the unemployed—but rarely ended there. Demonstrations brought people together, and in their numbers lay the seed of radicalisation. Strikes merged with speeches; placards denouncing poverty were soon joined by banners calling for revolution, reform, or revenge. In Berlin, clashes between communist and Nazi supporters turned unemployment marches into running battles. In Chicago, police cracked skulls as hunger marches demanded not only food but systemic change. The Depression revealed how swiftly the line between grievance and ideology could blur.

At a certain point, patience curdles into militancy. When hunger lingers too long, when governments remain deaf, when the sight of privilege persists beside mass destitution, some conclude that violence is the only language left. Weimar Germany supplied the starkest example: the unemployed filled the ranks of paramilitary groups, exchanging the boredom of idleness for the certainty of action. In the United States, too, the Bonus Army's march on Washington in 1932 showed how veterans, denied relief, could transform into a disciplined, angry force confronting the very government they had once served. Passive suffering hardened into confrontation, and confrontation threatened the very order that had failed to prevent it.

Public life fractured under the weight of scarcity. The shared civic square, where compromise and debate had once seemed possible, split into antagonistic blocs. Hunger and unemployment polarised communities into those who clung to the centre and those who demanded extremes. The middle ground, already fragile, eroded as people sought clarity in an age of confusion. Governments found themselves paralysed not only by economic constraints but by a public increasingly unwilling to grant them trust. The Depression turned parliaments into battlegrounds, rallies into spectacles, and city squares into contested territory where the future of democracy itself was at stake.

This chapter examines how hunger and joblessness remade the political landscape, not simply as social ills but as transformative forces. It is a story of breadlines that became symbols, of unemployment that hollowed out identity, of protests that morphed into ideological struggles, and of societies that, unable to find common ground, drifted toward barricades both literal and metaphorical. At its heart lies a question that still resonates: when economic systems fail, what holds societies together, and what drives them apart? The answer lies not only in policies and statistics but in the lived experience of deprivation—how it reshapes families, streets, and nations alike.

The breadlines and barricades of the 1930s remind us that scarcity does not merely wound the body; it remakes the political imagination. And as we turn to the case studies that follow, we see how the politics of hunger and the trauma of lost work did more than scar a generation—they redrew the map of global power and legitimacy.

The Politics of Hunger

In 1933, a reporter in Detroit described a sight that defied the mythology of America's boundless prosperity: families, once securely middle-class, waiting in line for bread alongside the destitute. Men who had worked in car factories, women who had once shopped with confidence, now stood silently, hats pulled low, waiting for a meal handed out by charity. Hunger had always existed at society's margins, but now it had moved into its centre, visible on every street corner. The paradox was impossible to ignore: warehouses still held food, farms still produced grain, yet millions starved or went malnourished. The hunger of the Depression was not born of absolute scarcity but of systemic failure—an indictment of governments that proved unable, or unwilling, to convert abundance into sustenance.

The breadline was never a neutral act of relief. It was a public humiliation, and at the same time a political theatre. Each queue outside a soup kitchen told a story: of states that had abdicated their responsibilities, of markets that had broken faith with their participants, of communities forced to rely on philanthropy rather than policy. In photographs circulated around the world, long queues appeared as mute parliaments of the dispossessed. They gave visual force to the abstract concept of government failure. When citizens stood in the cold for food, they also stood as living testimony to the inadequacy of democratic leadership.

The politics of hunger reached well beyond the question of diet. For families, scarcity destabilised the very foundations of life. Parents skipped meals so that children might eat, a quiet act of sacrifice repeated in millions of homes. Yet hunger's emotional weight could not be contained. Malnourishment bred illness; illness bred despair. Children sent to school hungry could not learn, perpetuating a cycle of hopelessness. Domestic tensions rose, marriages fractured, and the authority of parents weakened in households where providing the basics became impossible. In such environments, loyalty to government withered. How could a state that could not ensure bread claim to protect liberty or justice?

In the United States, Hoover's insistence that private charity would suffice only deepened resentment. Voluntary relief, impressive in scope, was never adequate to the scale of need. The spectacle of men waiting for handouts from churches or wealthy benefactors reinforced the perception that the federal government had abandoned its citizens. Hunger radicalised not only the unemployed but also the broader electorate, paving the way for Roosevelt's New Deal, which, whatever its economic efficacy, at least acknowledged the moral obligation of the state to intervene. Roosevelt's relief programmes did not simply feed people; they restored a sense that government was once again visible in the lives of ordinary citizens.

In Germany, the dynamic took a more sinister turn. Hunger there was tied not only to unemployment but also to the memory of post-war reparations and humiliation. The sight of impoverished families in cities like Berlin and Hamburg became potent symbols exploited by extremists. Nazi propaganda was filled with images of "forgotten Germans" betrayed by elites and international creditors. Food, or its absence, was used rhetorically as proof of a conspiracy: Jews, communists, and weak politicians were cast as culprits for the empty stomachs of the nation. Hunger did not produce Nazism, but it gave resonance to Hitler's promises of national renewal.

In Britain, hunger marches offered a different form of political indictment. When thousands of unemployed workers walked hundreds of miles to London in the early 1930s, they carried more than slogans; they carried their bodies as evidence of the government's neglect. The marches revealed the gap between the capital and the provinces, between policy and experience. They forced the spectacle of hunger into the heart of Westminster. Though officials often dismissed them, the marches changed public conversation, seeding debates about welfare, labour rights, and the responsibilities of the state that would bear fruit only after the war.

Hunger was also deeply divisive. For some, the sight of queues bred compassion and solidarity. For others, it bred resentment, the suspicion that the unemployed were lazy, undeserving, or even dangerous. Newspapers in every nation reflected these tensions: some called for compassion, others for crackdowns. Hunger thus became not just a humanitarian crisis but a battlefield of competing narratives about responsibility, morality, and power. The question of who deserved bread became inseparable from the question of who deserved citizenship.

The politics of hunger reveal a stark truth about democracy: legitimacy depends not on abstract principles but on the ability to provide basic security. Freedom of speech and fair elections mean little when citizens are starving. Hunger corrodes the foundations of civic trust faster than almost any other force, because it makes the failures of the state tangible in the body itself. A stomach that growls is not an ideological abstraction; it is a demand for relief that cannot be deferred.

Philosophically, hunger forces us to confront the relationship between rights and needs. Liberal democracies often defined themselves in terms of political freedoms, while leaving economic rights vague. The Depression exposed the fragility of that model. If the state could not guarantee sustenance, were its promises of liberty meaningful? Authoritarian movements exploited this gap by offering not freedom but bread—and for many, the trade felt justified. The lesson was as profound as it was unsettling: citizens will often exchange abstract liberties for the certainty of food.

The political weaponisation of hunger did not end with the Depression. Throughout the twentieth century, from Mao's China to Pinochet's Chile, regimes understood that controlling bread was as vital as controlling ballots. The 1930s were simply the most dramatic demonstration of how scarcity, when visible and prolonged, destabilises families and governments alike. Hunger is not just a biological condition; it is a political event.

The unresolved question, however, remains. Can democracies guarantee stability in the face of scarcity, or does hunger always tilt the scales toward authoritarian solutions? The breadlines of the Great Depression suggest that when the state fails to meet its most basic obligation, citizens do not simply grow hungry—they grow restless. And once hunger becomes political, the survival of democratic institutions themselves is on the table.

Unemployment as Identity Loss

On a grey morning in 1932, thousands of men filed into the Tiergarten in Berlin not to work, but to wait. They were not queuing for food or shelter, but for the daily ritual of registering their unemployment. The act was both bureaucratic and humiliating: stamping papers, collecting meagre benefits, then dispersing to idle streets and crowded cafés where others in the same condition lingered. What struck observers was not only the destitution but the sheer purposelessness of it all. These men had been mechanics, clerks, teachers, and labourers. Now they were reduced to a category: the unemployed. They carried not only empty wallets but hollowed identities.

Work in the industrial age had become more than a means of survival. It was a source of rhythm and structure, a mark of belonging in a society that increasingly defined people by their occupations. A shoemaker was not just a man who earned wages by crafting shoes; he was a shoemaker in the way a priest was a priest or a farmer a farmer. Occupation shaped pride, self-perception, and one's place in the hierarchy of community. When the Depression stripped millions of their jobs, it tore out the roots of this identity. Without work, people did not simply suffer material deprivation; they were cut loose from meaning.

The psychological cost was immense. In the United States, studies of unemployed men recorded feelings of worthlessness and shame so deep that many withdrew from family life, leaving wives to seek casual work or children to shoulder responsibility prematurely. Letters written to relief agencies often carried the same refrain: *I am not asking for charity, I want work.* The distinction mattered. Charity implied dependency, a loss of dignity. Work meant restored identity. This insistence reveals the extent to which employment functioned as a moral category as much as an economic one.

In Weimar Germany, the crisis was even sharper. The republic had inherited a culture of disciplined labour and professional pride, qualities that had survived the devastations of war and hyperinflation. To be denied work was not just hardship but dishonour. The unemployed filled cafés not out of leisure but desperation, waiting for news, finding solace in the company of others equally excluded from productivity. Political movements understood the vacuum they faced. Both communists and Nazis offered not only the promise of jobs but a reconstituted sense of purpose: in the class struggle, in the Volk, in the nation's destiny. Ideology provided a substitute identity where employment had failed.

The linkage between unemployment and radicalisation was not accidental. Deprived of the dignity of work, many sought belonging in groups that offered structure and meaning. Marching in formation, wearing uniforms, shouting slogans—these were activities that mirrored the lost rituals of labour: the discipline of the factory, the collective rhythm of the office or workshop. The unemployed who joined paramilitary units or mass rallies were not only voicing anger; they were reclaiming an identity. Extremist leaders understood this deeply. Hitler's speeches did not dwell only on economics; they dwelt on humiliation, purposelessness, the loss of dignity—and then promised restoration.

But even outside the orbit of radical movements, the loss of identity transformed societies. Families shifted as unemployed fathers ceded authority in households where mothers' resourcefulness or children's odd jobs kept families afloat. Traditional gender roles strained under the pressure, often provoking resentment or shame. In some cases, this reconfigured domestic life in ways that persisted long after the Depression ended. The cultural wound of unemployment reached far beyond the statistics of jobless men; it altered the very texture of family, community, and citizenship.

The philosophical implications are unsettling. Liberal democracies had long assumed that identity was grounded in individual rights and political freedoms. Yet the Depression revealed a harsher truth: for most, identity was grounded in work. Strip that away, and political freedoms lose their purchase. The unemployed man who cannot feed his family does not cling to the abstract dignity of voting rights; he longs for the concrete dignity of employment. This is why governments' failure to restore jobs felt not just like policy incompetence but like betrayal. And it is why extremist promises of full employment resonated even when they came shackled to authoritarianism.

Unemployment also tested the resilience of social solidarity. In the United States, the sight of men selling apples on street corners became a cliché of the Depression, yet behind the cliché was a quiet tragedy: each man isolated, competing for pennies in a society that measured worth by productivity. In Britain's industrial north, whole communities saw their collective identity unravel as mines and mills closed. Where once a town had been "a mining town" or "a shipbuilding town," it now became a place of remembered identity, living on pride in past work that no longer existed. A collective loss of occupation meant a collective loss of place.

There is an irony here worth underlining. Work had always been a source of exploitation as well as dignity. Long hours, dangerous conditions, and meagre wages had defined much of industrial labour. Yet when the Depression removed work altogether, people discovered that even exploited labour offered more identity than idleness. Better to be overworked than to be unwanted. This paradox points to a truth about human society: work, however oppressive, confers recognition, while unemployment confers invisibility. To be jobless was to be erased, a void in a world that measured existence by contribution.

The danger, of course, is that voids do not remain empty. Into them step ideologues with promises of belonging. Extremist parties across the world of the 1930s grasped this dynamic instinctively. They offered uniforms, slogans, and enemies to blame. They offered new identities where old ones had been stripped away. For many, this was not about ideology but survival of the self. To march was to be visible again; to wear a uniform was to recover dignity; to pledge loyalty was to regain worth.

The Depression thus forces us to ask: what happens to societies when millions lose not just income but meaning? The twentieth century offers a sobering answer: they become vulnerable to movements that redefine identity in collective, often destructive, terms. Unemployment did not merely destabilise economies; it destabilised the self. And when the self is destabilised, the ground is fertile for radical seeds.

The question remains unresolved, even now. In societies where work is again becoming precarious, where automation and globalisation displace millions, will the same dynamics resurface? Will the loss of occupational identity once more drive people toward movements that promise new solidarity, however authoritarian? The Depression warns us that the gravest danger of unemployment is not hunger alone but the emptiness it leaves in the human soul—and the forces eager to fill it.

Street Protests and Radical Voices

In the summer of 1932, Washington, D.C. was transformed into a camp of desperation. Tens of thousands of World War I veterans—many of them unemployed, many accompanied by wives and children—pitched tents and built makeshift shacks near the Capitol. They called themselves the Bonus Army, demanding early payment of the service bonuses promised years earlier. Their march began as a plea for justice, rooted in economic grievance. Yet as weeks passed and Congress resisted, the movement acquired a symbolic force larger than its demands. The government's decision to send in troops—bayonets fixed, tear gas deployed—to drive them out turned the camp into a battlefield. The Bonus Army had come for bread and dignity; it left behind a scar on American democracy and a potent reminder of how protest can mutate into radical confrontation.

The paradox of protest during the Great Depression was that it was rarely only about food or wages. The sight of hungry families marching in disciplined columns or striking workers occupying factories was at once a demand for survival and an assertion of political agency. When parliaments seemed paralysed and governments unresponsive, the street became the people's parliament. Crowds embodied solidarity that no petition could convey. And yet, precisely because protests channelled both suffering and hope, they attracted voices eager to push beyond immediate grievances toward sweeping ideological visions.

Nowhere was this clearer than in Germany. By 1930, with unemployment soaring into the millions, strikes and demonstrations filled Weimar's cities. Communists organised hunger marches that drew vast crowds, carrying banners proclaiming the collapse of capitalism and the inevitability of revolution. But they were not alone. The National Socialists mobilised their own parades, transforming rallies into spectacles of nationalist unity. To an unemployed metalworker, the choice between a red flag and a swastika might depend less on ideological conviction than on which march seemed to offer a sense of belonging, pride, and direction. The street was not neutral ground; it was a contested stage on which rival radicalisms performed for the loyalty of the desperate.

In Britain, the phenomenon took subtler but no less telling forms. The Great Depression hit hardest in the industrial north, where coal mines and shipyards closed and unemployment lingered for years. Hunger marches, most famously the Jarrow Crusade of 1936, turned local despair into national spectacle. Men walked hundreds of miles to London carrying petitions and banners, demanding work rather than charity. The marches were dignified, yet behind them lay a volatile undercurrent. Communist organisers frequently attached themselves to such movements, using the visibility of the protest to inject their critique of the capitalist system. The government's refusal to act decisively not only deepened the economic pain but also reinforced the perception that Westminster was detached from the lives of ordinary people.

Japan, too, saw its streets become politicised in the wake of export collapse. Falling silk prices ruined rural households, and protests erupted in both countryside and city. Student demonstrations often linked economic grievances to calls for national renewal through military expansion. The language of survival merged with nationalist rhetoric, turning discontent into justification for aggressive foreign policy. Where democratically minded leaders faltered, the military found a receptive audience in those for whom hunger had already dissolved faith in parliamentary compromise.

What tied these diverse movements together was the psychology of collective protest. Economic suffering is isolating: the unemployed man in his kitchen, the mother unable to feed her children, the worker watching his factory gates locked shut. Protest reversed that isolation. To march with thousands was to feel part of a community, to discover that one's private humiliation was a shared condition and therefore a political fact. This transformation—misery into solidarity, grievance into agency—was the alchemy of the Depression's street politics. But it was also perilous, for solidarity could be harnessed by competing radical voices who promised not just relief but revolution.

Governments often misjudged the significance of these movements. To dismiss them as disturbances or to repress them with force was to misunderstand their character. When Hoover's troops cleared the Bonus

Army camps, when Weimar police cracked down on protests, when Japanese authorities silenced demonstrators, they only confirmed what protesters already suspected: that existing institutions neither heard nor cared for them. Force hardened grievances into ideologies. Protests ceased to be pleas for relief and became evidence that only radical alternatives could deliver justice.

The philosophical resonance of Depression-era protests lies in what they reveal about democracy under strain. Liberal systems promise that grievances can be channelled through ballots, petitions, and debate. But when hunger stalks homes and unemployment strips identity, such channels appear intolerably slow. The urgency of the street becomes irresistible. In that urgency, democracy confronts its most serious test: can it adapt quickly enough to retain legitimacy, or will its delays and compromises yield the stage to those who offer clarity, certainty, and spectacle?

The voices that filled Depression streets were radical not because all participants began with radical intent, but because desperation is a solvent of moderation. Communists, fascists, and nationalists drew on the same well of disillusionment, shaping it into movements that promised not incremental change but sweeping transformation. What began as protests for bread often ended as votes for regimes that would soon demand blood.

The spectre of those protests lingers. Modern movements, too, often begin with economic grievances—against austerity, inequality, or precarious work—but can evolve into critiques of political legitimacy itself. The Depression reminds us that when governments fail to listen, protests do not merely fade; they are absorbed into the projects of those who can turn despair into ideology.

The unresolved tension of the 1930s still haunts us: can societies facing profound economic shocks preserve the fragile boundary between protest and radicalisation? Or will the hunger of the street once again be captured by voices that offer certainty in exchange for freedom? The answer, as the Depression revealed, is never foreordained—and always perilous to ignore.

From Desperation to Militancy

In the winter of 1932, Berlin's streets were no longer just thoroughfares for commuters and shoppers. They had become contested spaces patrolled by rival militias, each convinced that Germany's future would be secured not in parliament but through confrontation. Clashes between the Communist Party's Red Front Fighters and Nazi stormtroopers left bodies on the cobblestones, the violence normalised as part of daily life. It was a grim transformation: hunger marches had begun as pleas for bread, but now the language of politics was increasingly spoken through fists, truncheons, and revolvers. The boundary between desperation and militancy had been crossed.

The Great Depression produced countless victims resigned to endurance. Families queued at soup kitchens, workers waited in vain outside factory gates, and farmers faced the humiliation of foreclosure. Yet alongside resignation emerged another response—rebellion. When systems of relief seemed inadequate and political institutions paralysed, some abandoned patience altogether. Violence, once unthinkable for many, began to appear not only justifiable but necessary. The paradox of mass suffering is that while it immobilises some, it radicalises others, creating a combustible mixture of despair and defiance.

Why does hardship turn some towards quiet endurance and others towards militancy? Part of the answer lies in psychology. The collapse of employment or savings was not only material but existential: it stripped individuals of dignity, identity, and agency. For some, silence was intolerable. Joining a militant group, even at risk of death or imprisonment, restored a sense of purpose. Militancy was not born simply of hunger but of humiliation—the deeper injury of feeling ignored, powerless, and invisible.

Germany during the Depression offers the clearest case study. The collapse of credit after 1929 devastated a nation still scarred by the hyperinflation of the early 1920s. Millions, particularly among the young, faced a future with no employment, no stability, and no trust in democratic leaders. Street militias offered more than ideology; they offered belonging, uniforms, rituals, and the thrill of acting decisively in a paralysed society. To march in step, to fight an enemy—whether defined as capitalist exploiters or Marxist agitators—was to reclaim agency. In this sense, militancy was less about political conviction than about the psychology of empowerment.

Depression-era America never saw militias rise to the same prominence, yet violence still erupted when patience wore thin. Farmers in the Midwest, driven to ruin by collapsing crop prices and foreclosures, sometimes turned to direct action. Groups known as "penny auction" farmers would surround foreclosure sales, intimidating bidders to ensure land was sold back to its original owner for a token sum. These confrontations were not mass uprisings but symbolic rejections of a system perceived as cruel and indifferent. Elsewhere, unemployed councils—often linked to Communist organisers—faced off against police when trying to prevent evictions. The violence was sporadic and localised, but the impulse was familiar: when legality became indistinguishable from injustice, militancy seemed like a form of truth-telling.

The contrast between Germany and America highlights the importance of political context. In Weimar Germany, weak institutions and fragmented parties left no credible channel for grievances, and violence became the arena where politics advanced. In the United States, though militancy surfaced, democratic institutions—though strained—retained enough legitimacy to channel anger into reform rather than revolution. The difference illustrates that desperation alone does not produce militancy; it requires the collapse of confidence in systems of representation and the presence of movements willing to organise violence as a political tool.

Philosophically, this raises uncomfortable questions about the conditions under which violence acquires legitimacy in the minds of ordinary people. For liberal democracies, protest and petition are meant to suffice. Yet when economic catastrophe renders those tools impotent, violence can appear as the last form of speech available to the desperate. To reject violence entirely is to ignore the raw human need for agency; to embrace it is to risk the destruction of civic life. The Depression underscored how narrow the linc can be between a crowd seeking bread and a mob prepared to break windows or worse.

Militancy also carried its own psychological rewards. For those stripped of work and status, violence promised both catharsis and recognition. In the storm of combat—whether in a Berlin street brawl or a Midwest foreclosure battle—the individual felt seen, heard, and feared. Violence restored dignity by transforming victimhood into agency, however fleeting. Yet that dignity was often parasitic, feeding off the creation of enemies and the destruction of democratic compromise.

From a distance of nearly a century, it is tempting to see Depression-era militancy as a relic of a darker age. But the underlying dynamic—the transformation of desperation into militancy when institutions falter—remains with us. Economic crises still generate movements that oscillate between peaceful protest and violent confrontation. The Depression teaches us not to dismiss the shift as irrational but to understand it as deeply human. Where hunger and humiliation persist, where governments appear indifferent, violence will always have its appeal.

The unresolved question lingers: in moments of systemic failure, can societies create channels for agency that do not slide into militancy? Or is the pull of violence—its promise of dignity through defiance—an inescapable feature of human response to despair? The Great Depression suggests that the answer is perilously contingent, resting on the fragile legitimacy of institutions that must prove themselves in the darkest of times.

The Fractured Public Square

In times of prosperity, a public square can be a space of ordinary coexistence—vendors hawking their goods, families strolling, neighbours arguing but still listening. In times of collapse, the same square can harden into a battlefield of ideology, a theatre where compromise becomes not a virtue but a betrayal. During the Great Depression, hunger and unemployment did not simply erode individual lives; they reconfigured the very architecture of political life. Shared suffering did not unite, as optimists once hoped, but polarised. Citizens did not gather to solve problems collectively; they assembled in rival blocs, each convinced that only its vision could deliver salvation.

The paradox is striking. Economic hardship was universal: workers from left to right, rural or urban, white- or blue-collar, all endured some form of loss. Yet rather than forging solidarity, deprivation sharpened divisions. The unemployed did not see themselves as part of a single community of the dispossessed. Instead, they clustered around antagonistic explanations for their plight—some blaming bankers, others blaming communists, others immigrants or foreign powers. Hunger itself was mute; it required a narrative. And in the vacuum left by faltering democratic leadership, radicals supplied the loudest and most compelling stories.

Weimar Germany epitomised this fracturing. The Reichstag, already fragmented by proportional representation, became paralysed once economic collapse destroyed the credibility of centrist coalitions. Social Democrats warned that only solidarity could save democracy, while Communists declared that only revolution could. On the other side, Nazis insisted that Germany's wounds stemmed from traitors within and humiliation abroad. The common thread was that none believed compromise had meaning. The public square, once intended as a meeting place of citizens, became instead an arena of permanent antagonism. Those who still sought moderation appeared not virtuous but naïve.

The same dynamic played out, in less explosive form, in Britain and the United States. In Britain, hunger marches such as the famous Jarrow Crusade channelled despair into spectacle, but their reception revealed the divide: to some they were legitimate cries for justice, to others dangerous flirtations with subversion. In the United States, the Bonus Army's march on Washington in 1932 offered a dramatic display of unemployed veterans demanding early payment of promised benefits. When federal troops dispersed them with tear gas and bayonets, the image seared itself into national consciousness: the government confronting its own citizens as if they were a foreign enemy. The symbolism was devastating. Trust frayed; the square fractured.

Underlying these confrontations was the collapse of a shared grammar of legitimacy. Democracies rest not only on ballots but on habits of coexistence—an unspoken agreement that opponents are adversaries, not enemies. The Depression eroded this cultural glue. When hunger entered the home and unemployment persisted month after month, adversaries became scapegoats. Citizens ceased to imagine one another as partners in problem-solving and instead saw in their neighbour the embodiment of betrayal, privilege, or corruption. The square became not a space of dialogue but of accusation.

Philosophically, this raises an unsettling question: can democracy survive when compromise is equated with weakness? The Depression revealed the danger of binary thinking. To a starving family, the rhetoric of moderation often sounded like evasion. To those stripped of work and dignity, calls for patience seemed insulting. Extremists understood this instinctively. Their slogans were simple, their enemies clear, their promises immediate. Where democratic leaders preached prudence, radicals promised transformation. The allure was irresistible to many.

Yet not all societies fractured in the same way. America's constitutional system, despite its failings, still allowed Franklin Roosevelt to recast political legitimacy through the New Deal, reconstituting the square as a space of reform rather than insurrection. In Germany, no such recalibration was possible: once the centre collapsed, the extremes fed on each other, each confrontation deepening polarisation until compromise became unimaginable. This divergence underscores that the fracturing of public life is not automatic; it depends on how institutions and leaders manage despair.

The fractured square of the 1930s remains a warning. Economic crisis does not merely test material endurance; it tests the bonds that hold political communities together. When governments falter, hunger is politicised, unemployment weaponised, and compromise stigmatised. The public square, in theory the foundation of democracy, becomes instead its graveyard. The open question—still unresolved in our own time—is whether societies can repair the square once it breaks, or whether polarisation, once unleashed, follows its own inexorable logic toward domination by extremes. The Great Depression offers no simple answer, only the sobering reminder that the cohesion of public life is far more fragile than we often imagine.

Chapter 3

Germany: Democracy on Borrowed Time

On a cold January day in 1933, Adolf Hitler stood on the steps of the Reich Chancellery, newly appointed as Chancellor of Germany. To his supporters, it was the moment of national rebirth; to his detractors, a descent into political darkness. Yet the true story of how a fragile democracy unravelled cannot be told through that single moment. It must be traced back through a decade of financial instability, bitter resentments, and a republic built on foundations so brittle that a single economic earthquake could bring the whole edifice crashing down.

The Weimar Republic had always been a precarious experiment. Born not out of triumph but of defeat, it was the reluctant child of Versailles, burdened with reparations that stifled growth and branded as illegitimate by swathes of the political spectrum. Its first decade was marked by chaos: hyperinflation that turned savings into wallpaper, attempted coups from both right and left, and the constant suspicion that democracy was an imported costume rather than a native garment. By the mid-1920s, fragile stability seemed to return, propped up by American loans and international agreements. For a fleeting moment, cafés in Berlin buzzed with artistic ferment, and Germany gave the impression of a society re-anchoring itself. But the prosperity was thin, dependent, and easily disrupted.

When Wall Street imploded in 1929, the reverberations struck Germany harder than most. The Dawes Plan and later the Young Plan had tied the nation's recovery to the flow of American capital. As credit dried up, factories shuttered, banks collapsed, and unemployment spiralled. By 1932, one in three German workers was jobless. For those who had lived through hyperinflation only a decade earlier, the crisis revived a profound sense of betrayal: that the state was incapable of protecting its citizens, and that democracy was indistinguishable from weakness. Economic dependence, once hailed as a pragmatic bridge to recovery, now appeared as a chain binding the nation to forces beyond its control. Extremists wasted no time in hammering that message home.

In this climate, the rhetoric of radicals found fertile soil. The Nazis fused economic rage with nationalism, offering scapegoats in the form of Jews, communists, and the Versailles order itself. Hitler's speeches were choreographed performances of resentment and hope, weaving together the humiliation of unemployment with the promise of unity and revival. On the other side, communists declared that capitalism itself was rotten and that only revolution could save Germany from ruin. In the middle stood the centrist parties, hesitant, compromised, and increasingly irrelevant. Their appeals to reason could not match the raw emotional power of certainty offered by the extremes.

Each election became more than a contest of policies; it was a referendum on democracy itself. Voters did not merely choose parties; they chose between pluralism and authoritarianism, between patience and rupture. As support for moderate coalitions disintegrated, the very act of compromise became suspect. By the early 1930s, the Reichstag no longer functioned as a legislative chamber but as a stage for antagonism. Democracy's promise—to manage conflict within rules—collapsed under the weight of economic despair and political hatred.

This chapter explores how Weimar Germany's democratic institutions, already fragile, were undone by the Great Depression. It traces the trajectory from dependency on foreign loans to the collapse of economic sovereignty; from the disillusionment of citizens to the appeal of Hitler's rhetoric; from the erosion of centrist politics to the transformation of elections into existential choices. The German case is more than a tragic story of one nation. It is a warning about how quickly despair can turn ballots into weapons, and how fragile the idea of democracy remains when its legitimacy depends on prosperity.

As we proceed, the reader will see how Germany's crisis was not inevitable but contingent: shaped by decisions, failures, and the inability of institutions to adapt. At the heart of this chapter lies a question as relevant today as in 1930: what happens when democratic patience runs out, and people decide that waiting is no longer an option? The answers lie in the rise of Hitler, but the causes stretch far deeper—into the very fragility of a republic always living on borrowed time.

The Fragile Weimar Experiment

In November 1918, the guns of the First World War fell silent, but for Germany the armistice brought not peace but a profound identity crisis. The Kaiser was gone, revolutionaries roamed the streets of Berlin, and a new republic—christened in the city of Weimar rather than the capital itself for fear of unrest—was hurriedly assembled in the hope of preserving order. It was an experiment forced upon the nation rather than chosen by it, and from the outset its legitimacy was precarious. The Weimar Republic was not born out of victory or consensus, but out of defeat, resentment, and external imposition. This fragility would haunt every decision, every election, and every institution it sought to build.

The Versailles Treaty carved its terms into the new republic before its leaders had even settled into office. Territorial losses, disarmament, and the infamous Article 231—the "war guilt" clause—branded Germany as uniquely responsible for the catastrophe of 1914–1918. Reparations obligations stretched beyond economic capacity and were experienced as a daily humiliation. Even moderates who sought pragmatic cooperation with the Allied victors found themselves branded as "November criminals." The republic's enemies did not need to invent grievances; Versailles had written them into its very constitution.

Hyperinflation in the early 1920s deepened this wound. As the mark collapsed, wages and savings dissolved almost overnight. Middle-class families who had spent decades building modest security saw their life's work rendered worthless, while pensioners begged in the streets for food their stipends could no longer buy. The image of children playing with banknotes stacked like blocks became an enduring symbol of the absurdity and cruelty of the moment. Yet the psychological damage was more profound than the economic one: the belief that the state was capable of protecting its citizens evaporated. Institutions that rely on trust were stained permanently, and even when stability returned later in the decade, memories of betrayal lingered like an open wound.

The republic's political architecture compounded these vulnerabilities. Proportional representation, designed to ensure fairness, produced chronic instability. Cabinets rose and fell with dizzying frequency, coalitions stitched together more by necessity than conviction. The very mechanisms meant to express pluralism often paralysed governance. For those already sceptical of democracy, this dysfunction was not a regrettable side-effect but proof of democracy's inherent weakness. The republic was caught in a vicious cycle: instability undermined trust, which in turn produced more instability.

And yet, the mid-1920s briefly suggested another trajectory. With the Dawes Plan restructuring reparations and American loans fuelling investment, Germany experienced what some later called the "Golden Twenties." Berlin became a beacon of cultural modernism, a centre of art, literature, and avant-garde experimentation. For a moment, it seemed the republic might consolidate. But the stability was misleading, dependent on external credit and international goodwill. Beneath the surface, hostility remained entrenched: aristocratic elites and the army never fully accepted republican authority, while communists saw the system as a bourgeois betrayal. The Weimar Republic was a house standing, but never firmly rooted in its own soil.

The Great Depression exposed these weaknesses with ruthless clarity. When American capital retreated after 1929, the economic scaffolding holding up German recovery collapsed. Within three years, unemployment soared above six million, and despair reached into every class and region. For a people already scarred by hyperinflation, this second cataclysm confirmed a grim lesson: that democracy delivered not security but chaos. Extremists capitalised on this disillusionment with brutal efficiency, portraying the republic as incapable of shielding its citizens from either foreign humiliation or domestic catastrophe.

The fragility of the Weimar experiment forces us to reflect on the relationship between political form and cultural legitimacy. Can a democracy imposed from above, or born in defeat, ever truly thrive without deep-rooted consent? Germany's brief democratic interlude suggests how vulnerable institutions can be when they lack broad cultural anchorage. To govern effectively, the republic needed not only constitutions and elections but also faith, patience, and resilience among its citizens—qualities that had been battered by war, treaty, and inflation.

By the time the Depression struck, Weimar's institutions were already threadbare, unable to absorb the shock. The republic's fragility was not incidental; it was structural, the product of a foundation laid in resentment, humiliation, and mistrust. The tragedy was not simply that democracy collapsed in Germany, but that it had never truly been given the chance to stand on its own strength. The unresolved question, haunting then as now, is whether fragile democracies can ever endure prolonged crises—

or whether they are destined, under enough pressure, to give way to the certainties of authoritarianism.

Debt, Reparations, and Dependence

In the spring of 1931, queues formed not outside factories but outside shuttered banks. Germans rushed to withdraw what little remained of their savings after the collapse of Austria's Creditanstalt rippled across the continent. Within weeks, confidence in German banks evaporated, and the Reichsmark teetered on the brink of collapse. It was a crisis not made in Berlin, but in New York and Vienna—an indictment of just how little sovereignty Germany's recovery truly possessed. The very loans that had sustained prosperity in the 1920s became chains when Wall Street crumbled.

This paradox defined the Weimar Republic's economic existence: a nation forced to pay reparations to its former enemies while simultaneously dependent on those same enemies' financial systems to do so. The Dawes Plan of 1924 and its successor, the Young Plan of 1929, restructured Germany's reparations obligations and opened the floodgates of American credit. On paper, this looked like stability. American dollars rebuilt infrastructure, modernised industry, and underwrote the fragile currency. Berlin's cafés buzzed with cosmopolitan energy, department stores thrived, and unemployment briefly receded. Yet beneath the appearance of prosperity lay dependency of the most dangerous kind: an economy yoked to forces far beyond its control.

Reparations were more than an economic burden; they were a political scar. Every instalment sent abroad was experienced not merely as a financial transfer but as a moral humiliation, proof of Versailles' injustice and the republic's weakness. Extremist voices knew how to exploit this sentiment. Nationalists insisted that the payments were treasonous, evidence of politicians betraying the fatherland. Communists, by contrast, denounced them as a capitalist racket imposed by imperialist powers. What united the extremes was not their solutions but their contempt for the middle ground—an environment where moderates appeared compromised and powerless.

When the Great Depression struck, the fragile scaffolding collapsed. American lenders, themselves desperate for liquidity, called in loans and ceased new credit. German firms, reliant on this inflow to finance daily operations, cut production and dismissed workers. By 1932, six million Germans were unemployed, and the republic's carefully constructed illusion of stability lay in ruins. Dependency, once sold as pragmatism, now revealed itself as vulnerability. The rope that had pulled Germany forward also served as a noose when the global system buckled.

What made this dynamic especially volatile was the way dependency became ammunition in the political arena. Hitler's rhetoric fused economic grievance with nationalist outrage, presenting debt as enslavement. He derided the republic's leaders as puppets of foreign bankers, their signatures on reparations agreements proof of their betrayal. The Nazi promise was not simply to end unemployment but to restore sovereignty, to sever Germany's reliance on hostile creditors. This blend of economic despair and political humiliation proved intoxicating, especially to a populace that had already seen savings wiped out once before during hyperinflation.

It is tempting to ask whether Germany had any viable alternative. Without American loans in the 1920s, its recovery might never have begun. But the structure of dependence meant that Germany's fate was inseparable from the stability of the very powers that had defeated it. This was not partnership but subordination dressed as cooperation. The paradox of Weimar was that its survival required precisely the sort of external support that undermined its domestic legitimacy.

Dependency also reshaped the cultural imagination of politics. For many Germans, the republic itself came to symbolise weakness: a state that neither defended national honour nor provided economic security. In such conditions, it was not difficult for radicals to argue that democracy was not a remedy but the disease itself. The collapse of loans did more than crash banks; it crashed the idea that moderation could protect ordinary citizens.

The story of Germany's dependence in the 1920s and early 1930s is not merely a historical curiosity. It speaks to a recurring question: can a democracy survive if its prosperity is contingent upon forces beyond its control? The Weimar Republic shows how quickly interdependence can be reframed as submission, how loans can look like shackles, and how easily economic vulnerability can be weaponised by those who promise absolutes. When the global system falters, nations with fragile legitimacy face a brutal test. Germany failed that test—and the world paid the price.

The unresolved challenge remains: in times of crisis, does dependence strengthen cooperation, or does it sow the seeds of resentment that radicals will harvest? In Weimar, the answer was tragically clear, but it is a question that still echoes in every debate about global debt, sovereignty, and the political cost of economic reliance.

Nazi Rhetoric and Economic Rage

On a cold evening in January 1932, thousands crammed into a Munich beer hall, the air thick with cigarette smoke and anticipation. Adolf Hitler took the stage not as a statesman armed with policy, but as a performer who understood his audience's despair. He spoke not in the dry language of economics but in visceral images: broken families, empty factories, and hungry children betrayed by a corrupt elite and strangled by foreign creditors. Each phrase struck at wounds still raw from the Depression. Each pause allowed rage to swell into cheers. By the time he left the podium, the room was no longer a collection of unemployed workers and disillusioned veterans—it was a chorus united in indignation and ready to believe that their humiliation could be avenged.

The paradox of Hitler's appeal was that he had little to offer in concrete economic terms. His solutions were simplistic, often contradictory, and rarely feasible. Yet they resonated more powerfully than the carefully argued plans of moderates. Where others offered technical remedies, he offered enemies. Where others acknowledged complexity, he promised clarity. And in a time when millions had lost not just jobs but faith in the system itself, clarity felt like salvation.

Economic despair was the raw material; nationalist resentment was the mould into which Hitler poured it. He fused the trauma of the Depression with the unresolved humiliation of Versailles, insisting that Germany's suffering was not accidental but imposed. Reparations became proof of foreign exploitation, unemployment a consequence of betrayal, and inflation a symptom of Jewish manipulation. In this narrative, abstract market forces had faces, and despair had a culprit. The power of such rhetoric lay not in its factual accuracy—often it was wildly untrue—but in its emotional coherence. It gave suffering a story.

The emotional cadence of his speeches mattered as much as their content. Hitler mastered the rhythm of resentment, beginning with quiet sympathy, rising into anger, and climaxing in promises of redemption. He cast himself as both victim and saviour: the man who had suffered with his people and the leader uniquely capable of restoring their dignity. Crowds responded not just to his words but to the catharsis of shared fury, the sensation that their private anguish was now a public force.

What distinguished Nazi rhetoric from the grievances voiced by countless other politicians was its ability to collapse economic and cultural despair into a single identity crisis. The Depression was not framed merely as a failure of banks or politicians, but as a racial and national struggle. Germany, he claimed, was shackled by international financiers and undermined by internal enemies. The "Volk" were portrayed as virtuous, industrious, and unjustly oppressed; their liberation would come only by casting off both democratic weakness and alien corruption. Economic rage thus became the gateway to racialised nationalism.

This strategy was devastatingly effective because it transformed abstract frustration into tangible mobilisation. Unemployed men did not just hear explanations for their suffering—they were offered membership in a movement that promised meaning and belonging. Marching in uniform, raising arms in salute, chanting slogans: these acts turned despair into action, impotence into power. In a society where the middle ground had collapsed, this sense of solidarity was intoxicating.

Yet the success of Nazi rhetoric also exposed the limits of democratic resilience. Weimar's defenders struggled to counter such appeals because their discourse remained rooted in moderation and compromise. Economic despair is rarely appeased by incremental adjustments; it hungers for resolution. While centrist leaders debated tariffs and austerity, Hitler declared enemies and promised deliverance. The result was that rage found a home not in the institutions of democracy but in the rallies of extremism.

The legacy of this fusion of economic despair and nationalist resentment continues to resonate. It illustrates how crises of livelihood can be weaponised into crises of identity, and how the line between protest and mobilisation towards authoritarianism can be crossed almost imperceptibly. The danger is not only in what extremists say but in the emotional void they fill when others cannot.

The question that haunted Germany in 1932 remains pressing today: why do so many, when faced with hardship, prefer simple lies to difficult truths? Perhaps because rage feels less unbearable than despair, and scapegoats are easier to grasp than structural causes. The tragedy of Weimar was that too many found comfort in blame rather than in compromise. Whether modern societies fare better when economic storms return is a test that remains unresolved.

Collapse of the Centre

In the spring of 1930, Chancellor Hermann Müller's grand coalition fell apart over what might appear, at first glance, a minor dispute: how to finance unemployment insurance in a country gripped by mass joblessness. The Social Democrats favoured protecting workers through increased employer contributions; the conservative partners demanded cuts and austerity. Neither side would yield. What began as a technical quarrel became symptomatic of a deeper fracture. The coalition dissolved, and with it collapsed the last effective bulwark of parliamentary democracy in Weimar Germany. It was not the extremities that brought down the government that year, but the centre's inability to hold.

The paradox of Weimar politics was that its survival depended on compromise at precisely the moment when compromise was least tolerable. Economic crisis demands decisive action; yet the mechanics of coalition rule—shifting alliances, fragile partnerships, and endless negotiations—bred paralysis. The public, weary of inflation's scars and now battered by the Depression, saw dithering where they craved certainty. Each legislative stalemate chipped away at trust in the centre, making the appeals of radicals, with their clear and uncompromising visions, appear not only attractive but necessary.

The erosion of the centre was not simply a failure of political skill. It was also a failure of imagination. Centrist parties—the Social Democrats, the Centre Party, and the moderate liberals—remained wedded to a politics of incrementalism at a time when the ground beneath them was collapsing. They offered adjustments when the public demanded transformation. Their speeches appealed to proceduralism, fiscal responsibility, and cautious pragmatism—virtues in ordinary times, but in the throes of existential crisis, they came across as evasions. Against Hitler's fiery certainties and the Communists' promises of proletarian revolution, the centrists' half-measures sounded like defeat.

The consequences of this vacuum were most visible in the Reichstag elections. In 1928, the Social Democrats won the largest share of the vote and formed a broad coalition. Just two years later, they were unable to prevent the rise of Brüning's presidential government, which relied increasingly on emergency decrees issued by President Hindenburg. By 1932, parliamentary debate was little more than theatre. Each election no longer produced stable governance but merely a new scorecard of radical gains and centrist losses. Democracy, in effect, had been hollowed out from the inside, eroded not by a single coup but by the slow attrition of public faith.

This collapse of the centre highlights a deeper truth about political life: moderation is not self-sustaining. It thrives only when material stability grants people the luxury of patience. In times of acute hardship, moderation risks appearing as weakness, even cowardice. The Depression weaponised this perception. Radical parties exploited every instance of parliamentary deadlock to argue that only their uncompromising programmes could rescue the nation. The Nazis promised unity through strength, the Communists promised justice through class struggle, and both denounced the centre as corrupt, ineffectual, and complicit in national decline.

Yet it would be simplistic to say the centrists failed merely because of indecision. Their structural position was precarious from the outset. Weimar Germany was born out of defeat and humiliation, its political system imposed by Versailles and never fully legitimised in the eyes of many citizens. Centrist politicians were forced to defend institutions that much of the public regarded as imposed or illegitimate. They became guardians of a fragile order rather than champions of a compelling future. Without an inspiring narrative, their appeals to defend democracy sounded defensive rather than visionary.

The lesson resonates beyond Weimar. Democratic centres often struggle when pressed between extremes, particularly in moments of economic catastrophe. Their strength lies in balance and compromise, but when the very fabric of society feels torn, balance seems insufficient. People turn instead to movements that offer conviction, however dangerous, over caution, however reasonable. In this sense, the Weimar centre did not simply collapse—it was squeezed to death by the relentless pressure of crisis and the louder voices on either side.

The tragedy is that the centre's fall cleared the path for authoritarianism without a decisive battle. It dissolved not with an explosion but with a sigh, as voters abandoned it, leaders quarrelled among themselves, and institutions withered from neglect. The middle ground, once thought to be the safest place in politics, became a no-man's-land—empty, exposed, and fatally vulnerable.

The unresolved question, one that lingers across history and into the present, is whether the centre can ever truly withstand such storms. Can moderation find a language that inspires in times of desperation, or is it destined always to be drowned out by the certainties of the extremes? Weimar's fate suggests one answer, but history has yet to deliver its final verdict.

When Elections Turned Existential

On the morning of 14 September 1930, Germans queued outside polling stations in numbers unseen since the republic's founding. What might once have been a routine democratic exercise carried a sense of foreboding, as if every ballot dropped into the box carried the weight of national destiny. By nightfall, the results confirmed what many feared: the National Socialist German Workers' Party, dismissed as a fringe movement only two years earlier, had surged to become the second-largest party in the Reichstag. From that moment, German elections ceased to be merely about policies or coalitions; they became existential contests in which the very survival of democracy was on trial.

The paradox was stark. Elections are meant to strengthen democracy by renewing legitimacy. In Weimar, however, each election deepened the republic's fragility. Instead of stabilising governance, the act of voting fractured it further. Turnout was high, enthusiasm palpable, yet the consequence was not confidence in institutions but a growing sense that those institutions no longer mattered. Ballots became weapons wielded against the system itself, as citizens used democracy to vote away democracy.

Economic pain made politics combustible. The Great Depression tore through Germany with brutal efficiency: by 1932, one in three workers was unemployed, and those still in work often saw wages slashed. Amid such misery, electoral choices became expressions of despair and rage. Parties that once promised incremental reform appeared irrelevant, unable to stem the tide of suffering. Extremist parties, by contrast, spoke in absolutes. They did not offer half-measures but salvation—or revenge. To cast a vote for the Nazis or the Communists was not merely to prefer one tax policy over another; it was to demand the destruction of a system perceived as complicit in national humiliation and personal destitution.

The September 1930 elections marked a turning point, but the dynamic intensified with each subsequent contest. The presidential election of 1932 pitted the ageing Hindenburg against Hitler, transforming the campaign into a referendum on the republic's endurance. Hindenburg's victory seemed to offer respite, yet it was hollow. The vote did not resolve division but underscored it: nearly 13 million Germans had endorsed Hitler, granting his movement an aura of inevitability. Later that year, in the July Reichstag elections, the Nazis captured 37 per cent of the vote—an extraordinary leap in a parliamentary system designed to favour coalitions.

For millions of Germans, politics had ceased to be about governance and become a theatre of existential struggle.

Weimar's electoral crisis illustrates a critical psychological shift. Ordinary citizens, faced with collapsing livelihoods, began to perceive voting not as civic duty but as an act of self-defence. The ballot became a shield against hunger, a protest against humiliation, and in many cases, a sword to strike at enemies—real or imagined. Hitler's rhetoric of national rebirth through struggle dovetailed with this shift. He cast each election as a moment of destiny: the chance to save Germany from treachery, communism, and decline. In doing so, he redefined the meaning of the vote itself, transforming it into a plebiscite on whether Germany would live or die.

The centre parties, already weakened by internal fracture, were ill-equipped to meet this existential framing. Their campaigns spoke of stability, budgetary discipline, and incremental recovery. But to a public battered by unemployment and haunted by memories of hyperinflation, such appeals felt tone-deaf. When one is fighting for bread, compromise appears like betrayal. When one's dignity has been stripped away, patience feels like surrender. Against this backdrop, moderation became a political liability, and radicalism became synonymous with authenticity.

The breakdown of electoral normalcy raises a larger question: what happens when the mechanics of democracy accelerate its own destruction? In Weimar, the very frequency of elections—nine national votes between 1928 and 1933—undermined stability. Each ballot not only reshuffled power but also re-legitimised the radicals' claim that the system was failing. Elections, designed to provide continuity, instead created a cycle of perpetual crisis. With every vote, the stakes rose higher, until the choice was no longer between parties but between democracy itself and its abolition.

There is a haunting modern resonance in this transformation. Democracies across the world still assume that high voter turnout, competitive elections, and passionate campaigns signal health. Yet the Weimar experience reminds us that elections can become instruments of polarisation rather than renewal. When societies are wracked by inequality, humiliation, or fear, the ballot box may tempt citizens to gamble not on compromise but on rupture.

By 1933, the stakes had become unambiguous. The Reichstag elections of March that year—held under conditions of intimidation after the Reichstag fire—delivered the Nazis the momentum they needed to consolidate power. Voters who had once trusted in elections as a means of expression had, in effect, participated in their own disenfranchisement. The republic had not been overthrown by a coup from above but dismantled piece by piece through choices made at the polls.

The enduring question is whether this transformation was inevitable. Did the Depression make radicalisation unavoidable, or could visionary leadership and institutional resilience have preserved the centre? Weimar's tragedy lies not only in its collapse but in the uneasy knowledge that democracy's rituals—the very symbols of its vitality—became the instruments of its demise. Elections, far from safeguarding freedom, had turned existential. And once politics assumes that character, the survival of democracy hangs not on procedure but on whether citizens still believe it is worth defending.

Chapter 4

America: Liberty on Trial

In March 1933, as Franklin Delano Roosevelt prepared to take the oath of office, the United States was a nation on the brink. Banks had shuttered their doors in state after state; desperate depositors found themselves locked out, their savings frozen. Farmers abandoned fields to dust storms that rolled like dark seas across the Plains. Millions of men and women—proud veterans of an industrial boom—now queued at soup kitchens, their dignity traded for a ladle of broth. The country that had once styled itself the model of modern prosperity had become a theatre of despair. At stake was not only the American economy but the credibility of the democratic experiment itself.

The paradox was painful. America, long seen as the land of boundless opportunity, was paralysed by fear and inertia. President Herbert Hoover clung to the ethos of self-reliance, insisting that voluntary charity and individual grit could resolve the crisis. His reluctance to let the federal government intervene decisively reflected a deep-seated suspicion of state power. Yet this faith in restraint, admirable in more stable times, now appeared callous and out of step with the human catastrophe unfolding before him. As breadlines lengthened and banks crumbled, public patience with Hoover thinned. Confidence—the invisible glue that held both economy and polity together—was evaporating.

Into this void stepped Roosevelt, offering not certainty but courage. His promise of a "New Deal" was less a programme at first than a declaration of intent: that government would not stand idle, that it could and must act boldly. In this sense, Roosevelt's presidency marked a turning point not only in American politics but in the very philosophy of liberal democracy. Where Europe, battered by the Depression, increasingly turned to authoritarianism, the United States sought to rescue democracy by reimagining the state's role in economic life. Relief programmes, public works, and financial reforms became symbols of a new compact between citizens and their government—an implicit pledge that liberty would not mean abandonment.

Yet America's confrontation with the Depression was not fought in legislatures and banks alone. The Dust Bowl, a disaster of nature and human mismanagement, ravaged the heartland and drove tens of thousands westward in search of survival. Their plight was immortalised in John Steinbeck's prose and Dorothea Lange's haunting photographs—images that transformed suffering into collective memory. Music, too, carried the voice of despair and resilience: Woody Guthrie's ballads echoed with the rhythms of displacement and defiance. These cultural artefacts gave form to pain, preserving it as a moral record and embedding it within the national consciousness. They remind us that economic collapse is not merely measured in statistics but in lived experience, in families uprooted and identities reshaped.

If Roosevelt's policy innovations altered the machinery of government, his rhetoric transformed the atmosphere of public life. The banking crisis of 1933 is instructive. Facing a system-wide collapse, Roosevelt did not simply close banks temporarily; he spoke directly to the people through his now-famous fireside chats, explaining in plain, reassuring language what was at stake. In doing so, he reframed fear as a collective challenge rather than a solitary torment. Confidence returned not only because institutions stabilised but because citizens felt they were part of a shared effort. In this way, narrative itself became an instrument of reform.

Still, the American story was not one of unbroken triumph. Inequalities persisted, relief was uneven, and political battles raged over the limits of government action. Yet in comparative perspective, the endurance of American democracy during the Depression was remarkable. While Germany succumbed to Hitler and Japan to militarism, the United States stumbled but did not fall. Its democratic traditions bent under strain but did not snap. This resilience gave new substance to the idea of American exceptionalism, though it was tested as never before.

The stakes of this chapter are therefore immense. It traces how the Depression exposed the fragility of liberty in a nation that prided itself on strength, and how the response of leaders, citizens, and culture redefined the boundaries of democracy. It asks why America chose reform over authoritarianism, and whether that choice was the product of deep-rooted traditions, bold leadership, or mere historical contingency. Above all, it invites us to consider what liberty means when survival is at risk: whether freedom can endure when banks fail, fields turn to dust, and millions lose work.

The answers, as the chapter will show, are complex and contested. They speak to America's unique trajectory in the 1930s but also to enduring questions about the survival of democracy in times of crisis. For when liberty itself stands on trial, the verdict is never guaranteed.

The Hoover Years: Paralysis and Policy Drift

On the evening of 29 October 1929, the American president, Herbert Hoover, reportedly assured a group of anxious businessmen that "the fundamental business of the country... is on a sound and prosperous basis." His words, delivered the very day after Black Tuesday, now read less as reassurance and more as epitaph. Within months, the prosperity of the 1920s had dissolved into mass unemployment, collapsing banks, and paralysed trade. Yet Hoover, the engineer-president famed for his organisational brilliance in feeding millions of war-ravaged Europeans after 1918, proved peculiarly incapable of feeding his own people when famine of work and confidence engulfed the United States.

The paradox of Hoover lies precisely here. A man celebrated for humanitarian efficiency became the face of inertia. His instincts, forged in the culture of rugged individualism, resisted the idea that the federal government should intervene decisively in economic life. He feared that overreach would corrode the nation's moral fibre, making citizens dependent on state aid. To Hoover, economic collapse was a storm to be weathered with stoicism and voluntary cooperation, not a structural failure demanding radical reform. In the abstract, his reasoning was consistent with American tradition; in practice, it became a formula for paralysis.

Hoover's policy drift was not simply a failure of will but a clash of ideologies. He believed in the power of local charity, churches, and voluntary associations to care for the unemployed. Such faith had deep roots in American society, where self-help and civic responsibility were virtues woven into the national myth. Yet by 1931, when one in four Americans was jobless, soup kitchens run by private charities buckled under demand, and shanty towns—soon derisively dubbed "Hoovervilles"—sprang up in the shadow of city halls. The spectacle of destitution eroded not only confidence in the economy but trust in the very principles Hoover defended.

Economic orthodoxy compounded the paralysis. Hoover clung to balanced budgets and sound money, convinced that fiscal discipline was the surest path to recovery. His administration raised taxes and cut spending in the teeth of contraction, deepening the spiral. The Reconstruction Finance Corporation, established belatedly in 1932, offered loans to struggling banks and railroads but avoided direct relief to citizens, reinforcing the perception that Hoover's sympathies lay with institutions rather than people. Critics noted the irony: a president who had once marshalled American generosity for Belgian relief now appeared to withhold it from his own unemployed.

The psychological dimension of Hoover's response was equally significant. He feared that acknowledging the scale of disaster would incite panic, so he persisted in issuing optimistic statements even as conditions deteriorated. Yet the disconnect between presidential rhetoric and lived experience only sharpened disillusionment. The sight of veterans—men who had fought for the nation in 1917—camped in Washington during the Bonus March of 1932, demanding early payment of promised benefits, crystallised the sense of betrayal. When federal troops violently dispersed them, Hoover's moral authority collapsed alongside his political capital.

In fairness, Hoover was no caricature of indifference. He did attempt modest interventions: urging businesses to maintain wages, encouraging states to expand public works, and promoting international cooperation to stabilise currencies. But these measures were piecemeal, hesitant, and undercut by his own ideological brakes. Where boldness was required, caution prevailed. The net result was drift—an administration reactive rather than visionary, clinging to principles ill-suited to a crisis of unprecedented magnitude.

The deeper tragedy is that Hoover understood the scale of his dilemma more clearly than many contemporaries. Privately, he admitted that the Depression was unlike any previous downturn, global in scope and corrosive in effect. Yet he could not escape the intellectual straitjacket of his creed. He feared that radical state action would erode liberty, even as inaction corroded the legitimacy of democracy. In this sense, Hoover was not simply an individual failing but an emblem of America's ideological impasse: caught between the mythology of self-reliance and the emerging reality of systemic vulnerability.

The consequences of this paralysis extended beyond economics. By 1932, faith in democratic institutions was fraying. While America never descended into the extremism that consumed parts of Europe, the disillusionment Hoover deepened created fertile ground for political realignment. Franklin Roosevelt's triumph owed as much to Hoover's failures as to his own charisma. The contrast was stark: where Hoover embodied caution and drift, Roosevelt projected boldness and experimentation.

The Hoover years therefore mark more than a prelude to the New Deal. They illuminate a perennial tension within liberal democracies: how to balance individual liberty with collective security in times of crisis. Hoover's paralysis was not mere stubbornness; it was a symptom of a deeper dilemma—whether to cling to cherished ideals of independence or to adapt them to new realities of interdependence. That question, unresolved in Hoover's time, continues to haunt democracies faced with financial collapse, pandemics, and climate emergencies.

When a leader's creed prevents decisive action, does fidelity to principle become a vice rather than a virtue? Hoover's story suggests that ideals, however noble, can ossify into shackles if they resist adaptation. His presidency stands as a cautionary tale of how inaction, born of ideological conviction, can corrode public trust more swiftly than failure born of boldness. It forces us to ask: when crisis strikes, is drift more dangerous than error?

The Rise of Roosevelt's New Deal

On a damp March morning in 1933, crowds gathered outside shuttered banks across the United States. For months, confidence had evaporated: savings were withdrawn in panic, institutions collapsed, and with them the fragile belief that the future would be better than the present. When Franklin Delano Roosevelt stepped forward to take the oath of office, the nation was not simply mired in economic distress—it teetered on the brink of psychological despair. His first words as president, promising that "the only thing we have to fear is fear itself," were more than rhetoric. They were a calculated attempt to reframe crisis, to make fear itself the adversary and thus imply that courage could begin recovery. The words worked because they named what Americans felt most acutely: paralysis.

The paradox of Roosevelt's rise is that he came to power with no fixed blueprint for salvation. Unlike the ideologues of Europe—who offered manifestos, certainties, and enemies to blame—Roosevelt approached the crisis with a spirit of experimentation. "Bold, persistent experimentation," he called it. That openness was radical in its own way: he did not promise to preserve the old order intact, but neither did he seek to destroy it. Instead, he redefined the relationship between citizens and their state, not through abstract theories but through pragmatic programmes that put men to work, stabilised banks, and rekindled belief in government's capacity to act.

The New Deal was less a single plan than a rolling sequence of interventions, each crafted to address immediate dysfunctions while testing the boundaries of constitutional authority. The Emergency Banking Act reopened banks under federal supervision, restoring depositors' confidence almost overnight. The Civilian Conservation Corps recruited young men to plant trees, build trails, and reclaim farmland—providing not just wages but dignity in a time when idleness corroded the spirit. These programmes were more than economic relief: they were symbols that the state had ceased to be passive.

For farmers, devastated by dust storms and falling prices, the Agricultural Adjustment Administration sought to raise incomes by controlling production, a measure controversial yet transformative. For workers, the Wagner Act enshrined collective bargaining rights, fundamentally altering the balance of power between labour and capital. For the elderly and vulnerable, the Social Security Act of 1935 introduced the principle of guaranteed protection, embedding the idea that the state bore responsibility for its weakest members. Each of these measures, debated fiercely in Congress and the courts, incrementally redrew the boundaries of what democratic government could—and should—do.

Roosevelt's genius lay not only in policy design but in communication. His fireside chats, delivered by radio to millions of households, bypassed traditional elites and made politics intimate. Americans heard their president's voice in their living rooms, explaining complex banking reforms in plain language, asking for patience, urging faith. This rhetorical intimacy functioned as a counterpoint to the demagoguery rising elsewhere in the world. Where Mussolini shouted from balconies and Hitler mesmerised through rallies, Roosevelt spoke softly through the ether, persuading by trust rather than terror.

Critics, however, were legion. Conservatives accused him of edging toward socialism, undermining free enterprise with regulation and taxation. Business leaders chafed at labour protections, while the Supreme Court initially struck down several New Deal measures as unconstitutional overreach. On the other flank, radicals insisted Roosevelt had not gone nearly far enough—arguing that unemployment relief remained inadequate and wealth inequality unresolved. Figures like Huey Long in Louisiana gained traction by proposing even more redistributive schemes. Roosevelt navigated this turbulent middle ground, neither fully appeasing the left nor the right, but maintaining sufficient legitimacy to continue.

The international dimension is striking. While European nations slid toward authoritarian solutions, Roosevelt offered a democratic counter-example. He showed that a liberal democracy could mobilise state power on a vast scale without abandoning constitutional norms. The Tennessee Valley Authority, for instance, electrified rural communities, modernising whole regions without recourse to coercion. The Works Progress Administration funded not only bridges and roads but theatres, murals, and oral histories—an investment in culture as well as concrete. These projects became monuments to what a democracy, however embattled, could achieve without sacrificing liberty.

Yet the New Deal was not without contradictions. It often reinforced racial inequalities, with Black workers excluded from certain relief programmes or confined to segregated roles. Women, too, benefited unevenly, as many initiatives assumed the male breadwinner model. Moreover, Roosevelt's willingness to concentrate executive power set precedents that alarmed defenders of limited government. The New Deal, in retrospect, was both a lifeline and a leap into uncharted territory. It saved capitalism from collapse but also embedded expectations of federal responsibility that would permanently alter American politics.

What endures is the New Deal's psychological achievement. By making government visible—in the form of men building dams, artists painting murals, inspectors regulating banks—it restored faith that collective action was possible. At a time when despair threatened to fragment society, Roosevelt's programmes bound Americans together in a shared national project. The state ceased to be a distant arbiter and became a participant in daily survival.

Roosevelt's New Deal demonstrates that crisis can serve as a crucible, reshaping the boundaries of political imagination. The Depression did not produce a dictator in the United States, as it did in Germany, but it did produce a new settlement: one in which liberty was reinterpreted to include freedom from hunger, insecurity, and fear. Whether that redefinition strengthened democracy or tethered it to unsustainable promises remains an open question. What is clear is that Roosevelt's experiment transformed the trajectory of the republic—and in doing so, offered the world a reminder that democracy need not equate to drift.

But here lies the lingering tension: if democracy is saved by bold state intervention, does it cease to be the same democracy? Roosevelt himself left the answer deliberately ambiguous, framing his actions as both a defence of tradition and a revolution in government. The ambiguity endures, for each new crisis revives the question anew. How far can liberty bend to necessity before it breaks? Roosevelt's New Deal offered one answer; whether it remains sufficient for the crises of the present is another matter.

The Cultural Response: Dust Bowl to Dorothea Lange

In the spring of 1936, a photographer pulled her car to the side of a dusty California road. She had been documenting migrant camps for weeks, commissioned to capture the faces of those who had lost everything. There, outside a tattered tent, she found Florence Owens Thompson, a mother with her children clinging to her shoulders. Dorothea Lange lifted her camera, pressed the shutter, and produced one of the most iconic images of the twentieth century: *Migrant Mother*. In the lines etched across Thompson's face, the weight of hunger, endurance, and quiet defiance coalesced into a single portrait. The photograph would circulate widely, shaping how a nation understood its suffering. It remains a reminder that history is never only written in policies and speeches—it is also recorded in the cultural artefacts of those who endured.

The Great Depression was not only an economic catastrophe; it was a crisis of meaning. When livelihoods collapse, numbers on balance sheets fail to capture the human cost. Art, photography, and music became tools to bridge that gap, translating abstract statistics into emotional truth. The Dust Bowl, for instance, was both an environmental disaster and a cultural watershed. Millions of acres of farmland, stripped of topsoil by drought and poor agricultural practices, were transformed into barren wastelands. But it was not merely the land that dried up; so too did a sense of permanence and belonging. Families uprooted from Oklahoma, Texas, and Kansas carried their dislocation westward, and in the process they gave rise to songs, novels, and photographs that captured exile in real time.

John Steinbeck's *The Grapes of Wrath* distilled that experience into narrative form, following the Joad family as they migrated to California. Steinbeck's prose, grounded in journalistic observation, became literature with a moral charge. It accused a society that tolerated exploitation and indifference while millions starved. For many readers, Steinbeck gave words to an outrage they already felt but could not articulate. The novel was denounced by landowners as slander, yet its resonance lay precisely in that discomfort: it forced comfortable America to look into the eyes of the displaced.

Music, too, bore witness. Woody Guthrie, himself a child of the Dust Bowl, travelled with migrants, guitar in hand, chronicling the injustices of lost farms, broken promises, and government neglect. His ballads—sung in union halls, migrant camps, and on radio broadcasts—did not simply describe poverty; they turned grief into solidarity. Songs like "Do Re Mi" functioned as both warning and lament, reminding desperate families that California's promise of work often ended in disillusionment. Guthrie's lyrics remain powerful because they were lived testimony, sung from the perspective of those who had little but their voices.

Lange, along with other photographers working under the Farm Security Administration, helped construct what might be called the visual memory of the Depression. Roy Stryker, who directed the FSA's photography programme, insisted that the nation needed to *see* itself. His photographers captured tenant farmers in Mississippi, steelworkers in Pennsylvania, and migrant children in Arizona. Their images were disseminated in newspapers and exhibitions, embedding the Depression not as an abstract downturn but as a human crisis. These photographs blurred the line between documentation and activism: they were art intended to provoke empathy and, indirectly, policy.

This cultural flowering was not accidental. Roosevelt's New Deal included support for artists, writers, and performers through programmes such as the Federal Writers' Project and the Federal Theatre Project. These initiatives recognised that recovery was not only a matter of employment but of identity. A play staged in a small town, a mural painted on a post office wall, or a collection of folk songs gathered by fieldworkers—these acts of cultural labour affirmed that even in destitution, communities could produce meaning. Critics accused the projects of propaganda, but their endurance suggests something deeper: they gave a fractured nation stories in which to recognise itself.

What unites these disparate forms—novels, songs, photographs—is the search for dignity amid dispossession. The camera lens, the pen, the guitar string became instruments through which suffering was transformed into testimony. They also reveal a tension: cultural responses can both humanise and politicise. Steinbeck's novel was censored in some counties; Guthrie's songs alarmed conservatives who heard in them the seeds of socialism; Lange's photographs unsettled elites who preferred poverty remain invisible. Culture, in this sense, became an arena where democracy itself was contested, where truth was negotiated through art as much as through ballots.

Philosophically, the cultural artefacts of the Depression raise enduring questions. Why do societies in crisis turn to storytelling, image-making, and song? Perhaps because culture does more than record—it interprets. It helps individuals locate themselves within a larger narrative, offering a frame through which pain acquires meaning. For displaced farmers, Guthrie's songs offered not just lament but a sense that their suffering was shared. For readers of Steinbeck, outrage became collective responsibility. For viewers of Lange's photographs, private grief was transformed into public consciousness.

Yet culture also exposes fractures. The very need for Lange's *Migrant Mother* suggests that without visual proof, many Americans might have denied or minimised the suffering of migrants. The resistance to Steinbeck's novel reveals how threatening it can be to link economic collapse to systemic injustice rather than to personal failure. Culture comforts and confronts in equal measure. It consoles the afflicted but also unsettles the comfortable.

The legacy of these Depression-era cultural responses continues to shape how we remember economic crisis. When modern recessions strike, headlines often invoke images from the 1930s: breadlines, dust storms, migrant families. The visual and musical vocabulary forged during that decade became shorthand for collapse itself. But these artefacts remind us of something subtler: that cultural production is not a luxury in times of distress. It is essential, a means of preserving dignity and demanding recognition.

Still, one must ask: if culture helps societies make sense of collapse, does it also risk aestheticising suffering? Is there a danger that a photograph, however empathetic, freezes the poor as symbols rather than participants? Lange herself wrestled with this dilemma, later reflecting uneasily on the fame of *Migrant Mother*. Florence Thompson lived to express ambivalence, resenting that her image had circulated without her consent while her poverty remained unalleviated. This unresolved tension—the line between representation and exploitation—remains as relevant now as then.

In the end, the cultural response to the Depression demonstrates that history is not only about what governments do but about how ordinary people bear witness. The Dust Bowl migrants who carried guitars, the photographers who raised cameras, the writers who sharpened their pens—

all offered fragments of meaning in an age of collapse. Their work continues to remind us that when economies fail, humanity seeks expression. But whether expression alone is enough to prevent repetition—or whether it merely allows endurance until the next calamity—is a question left to each generation to answer anew.

Fear and Reform: Banking Crises as Turning Points

On a cold February morning in 1933, crowds gathered outside American banks, clutching savings books and cheques, demanding cash that was no longer there. The queues were quiet but tense, the silence broken only by the shuffle of feet and the occasional sob of someone turned away. Inside, bank tellers faced the impossible: vaults stripped bare, reserves exhausted, confidence shattered. By the time Franklin Roosevelt prepared to take office, the American banking system was paralysed—more than 4,000 banks had already collapsed, and governors in state after state declared "bank holidays" to stem the panic. What had begun as an economic downturn had metastasised into a psychological contagion: fear itself had become the crisis.

The paradox of the Depression-era banking collapse was that most banks were not insolvent at the moment depositors rushed to withdraw their savings. They failed because people believed they would fail. The financial system, so often presented as solid and mathematical, revealed its fragility: its foundations lay in collective trust. When that trust evaporated, numbers on ledgers became meaningless. What mattered was confidence—the invisible glue binding savers, lenders, and governments together. As Roosevelt would later remark, "the only thing we have to fear is fear itself." That phrase was no abstraction. It was the diagnosis of a crisis that was as much emotional as financial.

Banking collapses in the early 1930s illustrated the brutal feedback loop of fear. A rumour of instability was enough to spark a run. A run, once begun, created the very insolvency it anticipated. Banks that might otherwise have survived normal cycles of business were undone within hours. This dynamic exposed the limitations of Herbert Hoover's philosophy of voluntarism and self-reliance. In moments where collective psychology turned corrosive, moral exhortations to "remain calm" rang hollow. What was required was intervention—not only to stabilise balance sheets but to restore belief.

Roosevelt understood this intuitively. His decision to declare a nationwide "bank holiday" immediately after his inauguration in March 1933 was not just administrative. It was theatrical, a dramatic pause in the spiral of fear, giving his administration space to push through emergency legislation. But just as crucial was what followed: Roosevelt's first fireside chat, broadcast on the evening of 12 March. Speaking in plain language, without jargon or condescension, he explained to ordinary Americans how banks worked, why they had closed, and why they would reopen stronger. He framed depositors not as helpless victims but as participants in recovery, urging them to trust that their money would be safe. The following morning, when banks reopened, deposits exceeded withdrawals. In a single night, confidence was reborn.

The fireside chats exemplify how narrative can be a form of reform. Economic historians rightly stress the importance of legislation such as the Emergency Banking Act and the establishment of the Federal Deposit Insurance Corporation (FDIC). But laws alone could not repair faith. What Roosevelt achieved was a psychological reset, using the intimacy of radio to speak directly into American homes. By addressing fear with candour and reassurance, he converted panic into patience. The lesson is profound: crises of trust cannot be solved with policy alone—they require stories that reweave the social fabric.

This interplay of fear and reform was not unique to the United States. Banking crises across the globe during the Depression carried similar dynamics. In Austria, the collapse of the Creditanstalt bank in 1931 triggered an international panic, undermining currencies and fuelling political radicalisation. Yet unlike Roosevelt's America, Europe often lacked leaders who could pair reform with credible narrative. The absence of psychological reassurance compounded economic fragility, leaving space for extremists to step in with their own stories of betrayal and conspiracy. Where Roosevelt spoke of unity, others exploited division.

The American case therefore highlights a tension at the heart of democratic governance: can liberal institutions manage crises that are not merely technical but existential? Roosevelt's fireside chats were as much about defending democracy as they were about banking. By restoring trust in financial institutions, he also defended trust in government itself. The power of his words lay in their accessibility. Instead of abstract economic theory, he offered metaphors that made sense to ordinary citizens. Instead of secrecy, he offered transparency. In an age when authoritarian leaders across Europe promised certainty through control, Roosevelt promised stability through communication.

Yet the reliance on narrative raises deeper questions. Can trust built through words endure without structural reform? Roosevelt succeeded in part because his rhetoric was matched by tangible policy: deposit insurance, stricter regulation of banks, and public works that demonstrated government action. Without such substance, reassurance alone would have been hollow. Conversely, reform without reassurance might have been dismissed as another failed experiment. The fusion of the two—policy and narrative—was what marked 1933 as a turning point.

The episode also challenges the way we think about financial systems today. Markets and banks are often described in technical terms, as if their workings were detached from human psychology. Yet the Depression reminds us that fear and confidence are not peripheral—they are central. Numbers on a balance sheet may dictate solvency, but sentiment dictates survival. The collapse of trust can topple even the most carefully constructed institutions, while trust restored can revive them. In this sense, Roosevelt's fireside chats were not merely communication strategies; they were instruments of governance, wielded with as much significance as legislation or executive orders.

But the fragility of trust also exposes a vulnerability. If democratic leaders can use narrative to restore stability, what prevents demagogues from using narrative to destabilise it? Roosevelt's success depended on a reservoir of goodwill and the credibility of democratic institutions. In other contexts, stories of fear have been weaponised—bankers cast as conspirators, minorities blamed for collapse, foreign powers accused of sabotage. Narrative is a double-edged sword: it can bind a society together, but it can also fracture it. The Depression was a proving ground for both possibilities.

The image of queues outside shuttered banks in 1933 reminds us that economic crises are lived in moments of dread and uncertainty. The fireside chats remind us that leadership is measured not only by policies enacted but by the ability to speak to those fears without exploiting them. The Great Depression showed that the turning point in crisis is often not when the laws are passed or the banks reopen, but when people begin to believe again that tomorrow might be safer than today.

Still, an unsettling question lingers. If fear can unravel financial systems in days, and reform can restore them in weeks, what guarantees that stability will last? Is confidence ever more than a fragile truce between memory and hope? Roosevelt's moment of triumph suggests that narrative and reform together can hold chaos at bay. Yet it also reminds us that fear is never banished, only managed—and that the next collapse of trust may again demand voices capable of rebuilding faith from the ruins.

American Exceptionalism Tested

In 1932, as hunger marches rattled European capitals and street brawls between fascists and communists became a daily feature of public life, America faced its own reckoning. Unemployment soared to nearly a quarter of the workforce, farm foreclosures spread like wildfire, and banks collapsed by the thousands. The United States stood on the precipice of disintegration. Yet the Republic endured. While Germany abandoned parliamentary compromise and turned to dictatorship, while Italy doubled down on fascist corporatism, and while much of Central and Eastern Europe dissolved into authoritarian experiments, the United States chose a different path. The paradox was striking: the land most associated with unbridled capitalism weathered its greatest capitalist failure without abandoning democracy.

This resilience was not inevitable. The despair that fuelled extremist politics in Europe was also present in America: demagogues such as Father Charles Coughlin and Huey Long built vast followings by railing against bankers, elites, and the failures of government. Their rhetoric bore a striking resemblance to that of European agitators, promising radical redistribution or scapegoating shadowy conspiracies. Crowds of disillusioned citizens, battered by unemployment and hunger, were receptive. And yet, unlike Europe, these movements did not capture the state. The difference lay not in the absence of anger, but in the ability of American institutions—backed by Roosevelt's leadership—to absorb that anger, redirect it, and preserve the democratic framework.

At the heart of this endurance was the American constitutional tradition itself, with its peculiar blend of rigidity and flexibility. The separation of powers and federalist structure slowed radical ruptures, creating barriers to the seizure of total control. At the same time, Roosevelt's New Deal demonstrated a remarkable capacity for adaptation. By reimagining the role of the state—through public works, banking reform, and social safety nets—the system redefined itself without destroying itself. Europe, by contrast, found its institutions brittle, unable to bend without breaking. In Weimar Germany, paralysis of coalition politics left a vacuum that Hitler exploited. In Italy, liberal institutions collapsed under the weight of Mussolini's orchestrated violence. America's test was severe, but its structures bent rather than splintered.

Yet institutional design tells only part of the story. Equally important was cultural narrative. Roosevelt framed reform not as a repudiation of American tradition but as its fulfilment. Programmes such as the Civilian Conservation Corps or Social Security were cast as expressions of shared responsibility, not as revolutionary ruptures. The language of *renewal* rather than *revolution* allowed radical change to appear consistent with the American story of progress. Where European leaders cast democracy as weak and obsolete, Roosevelt presented it as resilient and self-correcting. In this sense, American exceptionalism was not about immunity to crisis but about the capacity to recast crisis as continuity.

The contrast with Europe was starkest in the political middle ground. In Germany, the centre collapsed under pressure, squeezed between communists on the left and Nazis on the right. In America, the Democratic Party under Roosevelt expanded into a broad coalition, holding together farmers, labourers, urban immigrants, and segments of the professional classes. This "New Deal coalition" did not eliminate conflict, but it prevented polarisation from collapsing into irreconcilable blocs. Where Europe fragmented into antagonistic camps, America constructed a tent large enough to contain them.

Nevertheless, the resilience of American democracy during the Depression must not be romanticised. The survival of institutions was not accompanied by universal inclusion. For African Americans, particularly in the South, the benefits of New Deal policies were uneven, often filtered through systems of racial exclusion. For many Mexican Americans, deportations under the guise of "repatriation" underscored the limits of solidarity. American exceptionalism in the 1930s was therefore selective, preserving democratic forms but leaving structural inequalities intact. Survival did not mean perfection—it meant postponing reckonings that would resurface in later decades.

The psychological element of resilience is also revealing. In Europe, the trauma of the First World War compounded the Depression, feeding narratives of betrayal and humiliation. In America, the memory of victory in 1918 fostered a different psychology: hardship was seen not as evidence of national weakness but as a temporary challenge. Roosevelt's fireside chats tapped into this sense of collective resilience, offering reassurance that suffering was shared and surmountable. The Depression became a trial of character as much as of economics. The language of testing—of democracy "on trial"—framed endurance itself as a patriotic act.

Still, the idea of American exceptionalism should be interrogated rather than accepted at face value. Was the United States truly unique in its democratic survival, or was it merely lucky in its geography and resources? Unlike Europe, America faced no hostile neighbours poised to exploit weakness. Unlike Germany, it bore no burden of reparations or territorial loss. Its vast internal market allowed for economic recovery less dependent on external trade. These structural advantages arguably cushioned the Republic, allowing democratic traditions to survive where others collapsed. Exceptionalism may therefore have been as much circumstance as character.

Yet this does not diminish the significance of the test. What matters is not only that democracy survived, but how it survived: through a mixture of institutional durability, cultural narrative, and political coalition-building. The Depression revealed democracy's vulnerability to collapse but also its capacity for reinvention. The American experience shows that survival is neither automatic nor guaranteed; it requires leadership willing to adapt and citizens willing to place trust, however fragile, in the promise of renewal.

And so the question lingers: was the United States' survival in the 1930s a testament to exceptional virtue, or merely to exceptional fortune? The answer may lie in the decades that followed. The institutions preserved during the Depression became the foundation for America's role as a global democratic power after 1945. Yet the fragility revealed in those years remains instructive. If democracy could be tested so severely once, what prevents another trial? Was exceptionalism a momentary reprieve, or a durable quality? The Great Depression left the question unresolved—inviting us to reflect on whether resilience is a permanent inheritance or a temporary grace.

Chapter 5

The Soviet Illusion

In the early 1930s, when breadlines lengthened across Chicago and Berlin, Moscow staged a different spectacle. Posters blazoned with images of heroic workers and smokestacks reaching into the sky proclaimed a society immune to capitalist collapse. Pravda declared that while bankers in the West toppled and parliaments floundered, the Soviet Union marched steadily forward, guided by the iron certainty of its Five-Year Plans. For a world mired in despair, this image of apparent stability—however constructed—was intoxicating.

The paradox was jarring. Here was a state born from revolution and civil war, its politics soaked in violence and its economy still scarred by backwardness, presenting itself as the model of modernity. While Wall Street unravelled and democracies dithered, Stalin's regime declared itself the one system untouched by the global crisis. It was a performance of immunity, a carefully staged drama in which propaganda substituted for prosperity. Yet many outside observers, desperate for alternatives, applauded. To some, the Soviet Union was not merely surviving—it was triumphing.

This illusion was crafted through the spectacle of mobilisation. The First Five-Year Plan, launched in 1928, promised to catapult a peasant nation into industrial power. When the Great Depression struck abroad, the contrast seemed stark: tractors rolled off Soviet assembly lines as factories closed in Detroit; Moscow paraded rising steel output while Pittsburgh shuttered plants. The narrative was clear—capitalism faltered, communism built. But behind the images of gleaming dams and new cities lay the grim reality of coercion. The drive for industrialisation was financed by the forced collectivisation of agriculture, a policy that tore apart the countryside and condemned millions to famine.

Yet it was precisely this juxtaposition—prosperity abroad proving illusory, suffering at home concealed—that gave the Soviet model its global allure. Intellectuals, travellers, and writers journeyed to Moscow and returned with rhapsodic accounts. George Bernard Shaw praised Soviet achievements with theatrical certainty; the American journalist Lincoln Steffens famously declared, "I have seen the future, and it works." For those battered by unemployment and the failures of liberal capitalism, such testimonies carried enormous weight. They fed a narrative that history itself was turning: the old world collapsing, the new one rising in the East.

The Depression amplified this mirage, making communism not just a domestic experiment but a global counter-narrative. Stalin's regime wielded the crisis abroad as proof of capitalism's bankruptcy. Propaganda emphasised the contrast: bread riots in London, bank runs in New York, and mass unemployment in Berlin set against Soviet claims of full employment and collective endeavour. To the disillusioned, the repression, censorship, and famine remained invisible—or excusable. What mattered was the promise of order in a world of chaos.

But the façade carried a darker truth. Stability in the Soviet Union was purchased at immense human cost. Famine in Ukraine and Kazakhstan killed millions, political purges decimated party ranks, and labour camps swelled with prisoners building the infrastructure of Stalin's "modernity." The world was shown photographs of Dnieperstroi, the great hydroelectric dam, while the bodies of those who perished constructing it were never displayed. The strength of the Soviet system lay not in immunity to crisis but in its capacity to conceal or suppress it.

The allure of the Soviet illusion forces us to confront a deeper question: why did so many thoughtful observers, confronted with evidence of repression, choose to believe in its promise? Part of the answer lies in the hunger for certainty during uncertain times. The Depression discredited the liberal faith in markets and cast doubt on parliamentary democracy. Against that backdrop, the image of a society marching in unison towards a defined goal seemed not only impressive but necessary. The appeal was psychological as much as ideological—the craving for direction when freedom seemed indistinguishable from chaos.

This chapter examines how the Depression was refracted through Moscow's lens: how propaganda created the illusion of immunity, how the Five-Year Plans became both an economic gamble and a political weapon, how the price of stability was measured in human suffering, and how the Soviet model captivated Western minds. It asks what happens when a society in crisis is offered the mirage of strength, and why illusions, once believed, can shape the course of global history as powerfully as material realities.

For while the Depression tested democracy in America and destroyed it in much of Europe, in the Soviet Union it fuelled a very different story—one of projection, persuasion, and endurance built on pain. To explore that illusion is to understand not only the choices of the 1930s but also the enduring danger of systems that trade freedom for certainty. And the question that remains unresolved, echoing across generations, is this: in times of collapse, do people prefer uncomfortable truths, or the seduction of stability—even if it is only an illusion?

The Depression Viewed from Moscow

In the early 1930s, while breadlines lengthened in Chicago and Berlin, Moscow's official newspapers proclaimed a triumph: "There is no crisis in the Soviet Union." At a time when Western economies convulsed under mass unemployment and collapsing credit, Soviet propaganda painted a picture of unstoppable industrial growth, new factories rising out of the steppe, and peasants marching joyfully towards collectivised abundance. The paradox was stark. The same decade that witnessed the Great Depression in capitalist countries was also presented as a decade of progress in the USSR. To many abroad, the spectacle appeared as living proof that communism had solved the riddle of economic instability.

For those peering across the ideological divide, the Depression seemed almost tailor-made for Soviet vindication. Bolshevik leaders had long insisted that capitalism was inherently crisis-prone, a system condemned to cycles of collapse. The Wall Street crash of 1929 appeared to confirm their warnings. The Soviet press described it as the inevitable implosion of a decadent order, while contrasting it with their own planned economy. Whether in *Pravda* or in posters plastered across factory walls, the message was relentlessly clear: where the West produced misery, Moscow produced steel, tractors, and certainty. This carefully curated image—part fact, part fiction—was not only for domestic consumption. It was designed to position the Soviet Union as history's rising power just as capitalism seemed to falter.

Yet beneath the surface, the story was far less simple. The Soviet Union in the early 1930s was itself in turmoil. Collectivisation had torn apart rural life, unleashing famine on a scale that killed millions, particularly in Ukraine. Industrialisation was pushed at breakneck speed, with workers driven by quotas that were as punishing as they were unrealistic. Still, the optics mattered. Photographs of gleaming new hydroelectric dams or model collective farms offered a counterpoint to the soup kitchens of Detroit. For a world searching for alternatives, the contrast could appear compelling, even if it was built on repression and silence.

The global reception to this dual narrative was striking. Western journalists, intellectuals, and travellers often returned with glowing accounts of Soviet vitality. Figures such as George Bernard Shaw and later, the American journalist Lincoln Steffens, famously declared that they had "seen the future, and it works." These testimonies did not merely reflect naïveté. They revealed the psychological hunger of a world desperate to believe that some system—any system—could tame economic chaos. To those battered by unemployment and political gridlock, Moscow's apparent dynamism seemed to offer lessons in discipline, planning, and unity.

Of course, the image of immunity was partly a mirage. The USSR was not insulated from global trade shocks; shortages of machinery, technical know-how, and food were constant. What it did have, however, was a political machinery capable of suppressing the signs of weakness. Famines were denied, protests silenced, and failures rebranded as sacrifices for future greatness. This capacity to control the narrative meant that even as millions starved, the Soviet state could project an aura of resilience unmatched by the fractured democracies of the West. It is here that the Depression reveals a deeper truth: survival in the age of crisis was not only about economics, but about perception, legitimacy, and the power to define reality.

The Depression, viewed from Moscow, thus offers a study in contrasts. For the Western world, it became a trauma that fuelled extremism, undermined trust, and tested democracy. For the Soviets, it was an opportunity to claim moral and ideological superiority, even as their own citizens paid the price for forced modernisation. The lesson, then, is not only about policy but about the political value of crisis. In an interconnected world, the ability to appear unshaken can matter as much as the ability to withstand the storm itself.

Yet this leaves a haunting question: what is the cost of resilience when it is built upon silence and suffering? If Moscow's illusion of stability helped communism gain credibility abroad, it also obscured the immense human toll beneath the façade. The Depression may have vindicated the Soviet system in the eyes of some, but it also demonstrated the enduring danger of mistaking strength for progress. The world's search for certainty, then as now, can blind it to the shadows behind the spectacle.

Five-Year Plans Amid Global Crisis

In 1928, as Wall Street prepared to scale new heights before its spectacular fall, Joseph Stalin launched an experiment that would transform the Soviet Union at breakneck speed. The First Five-Year Plan, announced with fanfare, promised to drag a largely agrarian empire into the ranks of industrial powers within half a decade. To achieve it, millions of peasants would be driven into collective farms, cities swollen with new industrial recruits, and resources funnelled into steel mills, coal pits, and tractor factories. The gamble was audacious. At the very moment capitalism was about to implode, Moscow wagered everything on the premise that economic destiny could be engineered, not endured.

What made the plan so striking was its defiance of the prevailing mood abroad. In London, New York, and Berlin, political leaders hesitated, constrained by market logics and electoral pressures, paralysed as economies shrank and unemployment soared. By contrast, the Soviet leadership projected decisiveness. Targets were announced with military precision: coal production to triple, steel output to quadruple, vast new cities like Magnitogorsk to rise from empty plains. The Depression seemed to prove the superiority of command over chaos, of mobilisation over drift. Stalin was not merely building factories—he was crafting a political weapon, using industrialisation to showcase the strength of authoritarian resolve in a world paralysed by doubt.

The statistics, even when inflated by propaganda, conveyed the scale of transformation. In the space of a few years, the Soviet Union leapt from relative backwardness to becoming the world's second-largest industrial power. Electricity output multiplied, rail networks expanded, and production of tractors and tanks surged. These were not abstract figures; they were staged as visible symbols of modernity. Towering smokestacks, roaring turbines, and mechanised farms became part of the Soviet iconography, set against Western images of shuttered factories and breadlines. The industrial drive was not only economic policy—it was a theatre of power.

Yet the human cost was staggering. Millions of peasants resisted collectivisation, slaughtering livestock rather than surrendering them to state farms. Famine followed, most infamously in Ukraine, where starvation was weaponised against perceived "kulak" resistance. Industrial workers faced punishing quotas, unsafe conditions, and harsh punishments for failure. The "success" of the Five-Year Plans was thus bought with extraordinary sacrifice, enforced by coercion and repression. But this was precisely the point: Stalin's modernisation strategy was designed not just to build industry, but to forge discipline, to demonstrate that the state could bend society to its will.

This combination of progress and brutality confounded observers abroad. To Western intellectuals disillusioned by the Depression, the Soviet model seemed to offer proof that economic collapse was not inevitable, that a strong state could chart its own path. Figures from the British left to American progressives marvelled at the apparent dynamism. Soviet propaganda tours carefully choreographed visits to showcase model factories and bustling collective farms, concealing the famine and coercion. Visitors left with images of energy and purpose, contrasting sharply with the inertia of their home governments.

Yet the very centralisation that made mobilisation possible carried inherent risks. Targets were often fantastical, production figures falsified to meet them, and resources misallocated in pursuit of political prestige. The rush to industrialise created bottlenecks and inefficiencies, and the emphasis on heavy industry came at the expense of consumer goods. But in a decade when Western economies collapsed, the Soviet Union's visible growth—however uneven—was enough to project a sense of resilience. The gamble had succeeded in its primary objective: convincing the world, and many of its own citizens, that communism offered a path to strength in a century defined by crisis.

The Five-Year Plans thus represented more than an economic programme. They were an assertion of ideological confidence at a moment when capitalism looked discredited. Where liberal governments appeared paralysed, the Kremlin embodied motion. Where democracies hesitated, Stalin's regime declared certainty. The Depression gave the plans their global resonance, transforming them from domestic policy into a spectacle of defiance against capitalist weakness.

But the question remains: can economic vitality be measured in steel tonnage alone, if achieved through famine, fear, and silence? The Soviet Union's industrial surge impressed the world, yet its human toll was systematically erased from the narrative. In the shadow of capitalist collapse, authoritarianism seemed to promise stability and progress. What the Five-Year Plans ultimately revealed was not just the malleability of economies under compulsion, but the fragility of societies willing to believe that power and prosperity can be built on suffering without consequence.

The Price of Stability

In the early 1930s, Soviet leaders boasted that their country had defied the global Depression. While Wall Street brokers leapt from windows and German workers queued for bread, Moscow proclaimed steady growth, rising steel output, and an economy insulated from the chaos of capitalism. To the outside world, it appeared a paradox: a system often derided as unworkable was, at least on the surface, thriving while the free market crumbled. Yet behind this façade of stability lay one of the darkest human costs of the twentieth century. What kept the Soviet machine moving was not an absence of crisis but its concealment, enforced by terror, silence, and famine.

Few images capture this contradiction more sharply than the photographs smuggled out of Ukraine during the Holodomor of 1932–33. In cities like Kharkiv, shop windows displayed posters trumpeting record harvests while peasants collapsed from hunger in the streets. Trains laden with grain departed for export, even as villages starved under requisition quotas so severe that families were stripped of seed reserves and foodstuffs. To admit the famine was to confess weakness. So it was denied, even as millions perished. The "stability" the Soviet Union projected was sustained through mass death, rationalised as the necessary price of modernisation and control.

This logic extended beyond the fields. Industrial workers faced draconian demands to meet production targets, with failure criminalised as "sabotage." The prison camps of the Gulag expanded rapidly, providing a captive labour force for mines, logging camps, and remote industrial projects. Those who resisted collectivisation, questioned quotas, or even told jokes at the wrong time could be denounced, arrested, and disappeared. Stability was manufactured not by consensus but by fear: a system in which dissent was rendered unthinkable and suffering was reframed as sacrifice for the collective future.

And yet, paradoxically, the repression worked in projecting resilience. To many in the West, unaware of the full scale of famine or gulags, the Soviet Union looked disciplined, energetic, and purposeful. While parliaments elsewhere fractured over austerity, Moscow seemed decisive. Writers such as George Bernard Shaw and Sidney and Beatrice Webb visited in these years and reported glowingly of bustling factories and new housing projects, persuaded by carefully staged tours. The repression that made such achievements possible remained largely invisible. This selective vision helped sustain the illusion of a state immune to the convulsions of capitalism.

But repression was not simply a mask; it was a tool of governance. The purges and show trials of the later 1930s, with their theatrical confessions and choreographed denunciations, reinforced the message that individuals were expendable, but the system endured. The destruction of "enemies of the people" became a ritual performance of stability, a way of explaining away any failure or shortfall. Blame was shifted onto saboteurs and spies, never onto the structure of command itself. Stability was thus not the absence of disruption but the perpetual management of crisis through violence.

The cost of this approach, however, was profound. By suppressing independent initiative, terror undermined the very dynamism it claimed to defend. Agricultural productivity stagnated, scientific work was distorted by ideological conformity, and an entire society was trained to hide truth rather than confront it. Yet, in the short term, repression insulated the regime. Where democracies risked collapse under the pressure of economic pain, the Soviet Union could enforce endurance, however brutal. In this sense, stability was not a natural state but an artefact of power—the ability to decide who lived, who starved, and who vanished into the camps.

The wider lesson of this period is unsettling. Stability, when measured only by the absence of open revolt, can conceal extraordinary violence. The Soviet Union of the 1930s appeared composed to outsiders precisely because fear eliminated visible alternatives. But beneath the still surface lay a society convulsed by hunger, mourning, and unspoken grief. The Depression exposed the fragility of capitalist economies; Stalin's response exposed the fragility of human dignity when subordinated to authoritarian imperatives.

The paradox remains unresolved: is a society truly stable if that stability depends on silence enforced by death? For a time, the Soviet Union convinced both its citizens and many foreign observers that the answer was yes. But history invites a harsher question—whether such stability is ever more than an illusion, destined eventually to fracture under the very human suffering it suppresses.

Western Intellectuals and the Soviet Mirage

In the depths of the Great Depression, when the streets of New York were crowded with unemployed men selling apples for pennies and Germany seethed with the anger that would propel extremism to power, a curious stream of Western intellectuals journeyed eastwards. They did not travel to Paris or London for reassurance but to Moscow, seeking in the Soviet Union a glimpse of the future. Many returned with glowing reports of a land free from unemployment, where factories hummed with activity and poverty had been abolished by collective effort. For those wearied by capitalism's failures, these testimonies carried the weight of revelation. The paradox was striking: some of the keenest critical minds of the West suspended disbelief when confronted with Stalin's carefully orchestrated spectacle.

Among them were luminaries such as George Bernard Shaw, the Webbs, and the American journalist Lincoln Steffens, who famously proclaimed after visiting Russia in 1919, *"I have seen the future, and it works."* Even when later travellers passed through during the hunger and repression of the 1930s, many remained enchanted. Their descriptions were not fabrications, at least not entirely—they had seen new schools, vast construction sites, workers being feted as heroes. What they had not seen, or chose not to see, were the labour camps swelling across Siberia, the starving villages of Ukraine, or the culture of fear that silenced dissent. The Soviet Union excelled at stage-managing visitors' impressions. Tours were curated, conversations rehearsed, statistics polished. The illusion was both deliberate and, for many, persuasive.

Why were such figures so susceptible? Part of the answer lies in the political and moral exhaustion of their own societies. Capitalist democracies appeared rudderless in the early 1930s, paralysed by unemployment, strikes, and political stalemate. To intellectuals who longed for decisive action, the Soviet Union offered the spectacle of purposeful mobilisation. The Five-Year Plans projected scale, ambition, and momentum—qualities starkly absent from Washington or Westminster. For writers steeped in the rhetoric of progress, the USSR seemed to have turned slogans into steel. It was, to borrow a phrase often used at the time, *history on the march.*

There was also an emotional dimension. Many Western observers wanted to believe. The Depression had corroded faith not only in economics but in meaning: the promise that liberal democracy guaranteed improvement appeared threadbare. The Soviet Union, by contrast, seemed to offer a moral narrative—a vision of shared sacrifice for collective uplift. Intellectuals, particularly those with socialist sympathies, often found themselves moved not simply by statistics but by symbols: the worker elevated as hero, the factory celebrated as cathedral, the state committed to remaking society itself. The allure of this imagery was not easily dispelled by rumours of repression.

Yet not all voices were uncritical. Writers like André Gide, who initially admired the Soviet experiment, returned from visits profoundly disillusioned. Gide described the atmosphere of fear, the censorship, and the suffocating uniformity of thought. He was denounced by pro-Soviet circles for his betrayal, but his testimony exposed the rift between the utopian narrative and the lived reality. Others, like Malcolm Muggeridge and Gareth Jones, reported on the famine in Ukraine, only to face vilification by colleagues and pressure from Soviet sympathisers in the West. These contrasting responses reveal the power of ideology to shape perception: some saw only what confirmed their hopes, while others forced themselves to confront what unsettled them.

The Soviet mirage also underscores a larger philosophical question: why do societies in crisis become receptive to strong-state promises? Intellectuals are not immune to the seductions of order, certainty, and apparent purpose. When capitalism appeared to be collapsing under its contradictions, the Soviet model seemed to offer not just an alternative economy but an alternative civilisation. To admire the USSR was, in many cases, less about endorsing Stalin's purges than about rejecting the inertia of parliaments and markets back home. The dream of a society remade by design had a gravitational pull that facts alone could not counterbalance.

The consequences of this enchantment were far-reaching. Positive portrayals by respected writers and travellers helped legitimise the Soviet Union abroad, lending it credibility at a time when its domestic policies inflicted immense suffering. At universities and in political movements, the Soviet example inspired new currents of thought, from earnest socialism to militant communism. Even when the brutality of Stalin's rule became undeniable, the earlier praise left an enduring mark: the idea that authoritarian strength might succeed where democracy faltered.

What is perhaps most unsettling is how familiar the pattern feels. In moments of uncertainty, when democratic systems appear paralysed and inequality glaring, the attraction of models that promise decisiveness and clarity grows stronger. The Soviet mirage reminds us not only of the illusions others once embraced but of the vulnerabilities that persist in societies today. For the mirage was never simply about Moscow; it was also about the gaze of outsiders, their hopes and fears refracted through the image of a system that seemed to embody resolve.

The Soviet Union ultimately revealed itself less as a utopia than as a cautionary tale, but the testimonies of those Western intellectuals remain a window into how fragile conviction can be when disillusionment spreads. The question lingers still: when faced with crisis, do we look hardest at uncomfortable truths, or do we, like so many of those visitors, prefer the comfort of illusions that promise certainty?

Communism as a Global Counter-Narrative

In the winter of 1931, unemployed men marched through the streets of Chicago, carrying placards not for work but for revolution. "*We want bread, not speeches!*" they chanted, borrowing slogans from far beyond America's shores. For observers at the time, it was startling. A creed born in the industrial districts of 19th-century Europe and hardened in the crucible of Bolshevik revolution was now finding resonance in the world's largest capitalist democracy. The paradox was plain: the more capitalism faltered, the more communism, once dismissed as a fringe dogma, seemed to offer both an explanation and an alternative.

The Great Depression magnified this appeal. Across continents, capitalism's legitimacy appeared to collapse alongside its banks and factories. Entire societies saw unemployment rates climb beyond 30 per cent, farmers dumped food while urban families starved, and governments responded with halting or contradictory policies. Communists, by contrast, offered certainty. They insisted the crisis was not an accident of mismanagement but proof of capitalism's structural failure, a terminal illness rather than a temporary fever. For the first time, this argument resonated not only among workers on the margins but also within the middle classes and among intellectuals who had once viewed Marxism as little more than utopian theory.

The Soviet Union seized this moment with ruthless skill. It projected itself as the only nation immune to the catastrophe engulfing the West. Moscow's propaganda machine proclaimed: *no unemployment, no breadlines, no bankruptcies.* The message travelled through films, pamphlets, travelling exhibitions, and the glowing accounts of sympathetic visitors. At a time when American farmers abandoned their land and German children begged in the streets, the image of a worker in Moscow striding confidently into a gleaming new factory carried immense symbolic power. Whatever the hidden costs—forced collectivisation, famine, gulags—abroad the narrative was one of stability and forward momentum.

This ideological battlefield extended deep into Western societies. Communist parties in France, Britain, and the United States grew significantly in membership during the Depression years. The Communist Party USA, though never a mass movement, gained visibility by organising hunger marches, leading eviction protests, and defending the Scottsboro Boys, an emblematic case of racial injustice. These actions gave communists a presence in struggles that mainstream political parties often ignored. In France, the Popular Front coalition, heavily influenced by communists, came to power in 1936, introducing sweeping labour reforms. In Spain, communism became entangled in the bloody struggle of the Civil War, where Soviet aid shaped the fate of the Republic.

The expansion of communism's reach, however, was not only political but intellectual. Writers, artists, and students debated its ideas with urgency. The Depression had shattered the assumption that liberal democracy and free markets naturally ensured progress. Communism, by contrast, appeared to offer a coherent worldview: history as a struggle, capitalism as a doomed stage, socialism as the next step. For many, this narrative gave order to chaos, transforming individual despair into collective purpose. The appeal was not merely economic but existential—a promise that suffering could be redeemed within a larger movement of history.

Still, the counter-narrative was fraught with contradictions. Communism's critics pointed to the violence, censorship, and repression within the Soviet Union, warning that the cost of stability was freedom itself. Trotskyists, anarchists, and even disillusioned communists exposed the gulags and purges, insisting that the Soviet model betrayed the emancipatory ideals it claimed to embody. Yet the fact that such revelations could be dismissed by so many demonstrates the depth of the crisis: when people lose faith in their own systems, even brutal alternatives can appear attractive.

The Depression, therefore, did not create communism, but it did globalise its relevance. It forced millions to ask questions that liberal democracies had evaded: What happens when markets fail utterly? Can democracy survive mass unemployment? Is there a system capable of guaranteeing security in the face of collapse? For some, communism was not a final answer but a weapon—a means of pressuring existing governments into reform. The New Deal in the United States and the Popular Front in France, for example, can partly be understood as democratic responses made urgent by the spectre of communist alternatives.

Seen from today, this period offers more than a historical curiosity. It is a reminder that ideas gain traction not only through their intrinsic merit but through the failures of their rivals. Communism's rise as a global counter-narrative was as much about the discrediting of capitalism as about the achievements of Moscow. The shadow it cast reshaped politics, labour movements, and intellectual life across continents.

Yet the enduring question remains: what do societies do when their dominant systems no longer command belief? The Depression showed that in moments of profound crisis, counter-narratives gain not only credibility but urgency, and people who once dismissed them as radical or dangerous may embrace them as necessary. The allure of certainty in uncertain times is timeless. The only variable is which ideology—old or new—steps forward to claim the role of salvation.

Chapter 6

Japan: Militarism and Markets

In the autumn of 1931, a group of Japanese officers staged a carefully engineered explosion on a railway track outside Mukden in Manchuria. The blast was minor, almost farcical in its execution, but its consequences were seismic. Within hours, the Japanese Kwantung Army launched a full-scale invasion, bypassing Tokyo's civilian authorities and reshaping East Asia's political landscape. The "Manchurian Incident" revealed more than military audacity; it exposed the vulnerability of a political order hollowed out by economic collapse. What appeared a local skirmish was in truth a symptom of something larger—the conversion of economic despair into imperial ambition.

The paradox of Japan during the Great Depression is stark. Unlike the United States or Germany, it did not face total industrial ruin. Yet its vulnerability was acute: an island nation with scarce natural resources, tethered to global markets, and dependent on the sale of silk abroad. When the price of silk collapsed in 1929, rural households disintegrated, farmers sold daughters into servitude, and suicides spiked. The shock reverberated through cities as well, where unemployment and hunger fuelled resentment against politicians who seemed powerless. In that vacuum, the military presented itself not merely as a defender of national honour but as the guarantor of economic survival.

What made Japan's trajectory distinctive was the fusion of nationalism with economic policy. Expansionism was framed not as aggression but as necessity. Manchuria was marketed as a "lifeline," a promised land rich in coal, iron, and farmland, a solution to Japan's twin crises of scarcity and unemployment. For the militarists, conquest was not an alternative to economic modernisation; it *was* modernisation, pursued with bayonets rather than balance sheets. The argument was seductive precisely because the civilian leadership offered no coherent counter-vision. Where Western democracies experimented with welfare or regulation, Japan's rulers doubled down on empire.

This chapter examines how an economic downturn became the crucible for authoritarian advance. It traces the interplay between markets and militarism: the collapse of export-led prosperity, the delegitimisation of parliamentary politics, and the translation of economic desperation into geopolitical aggression. Each development illuminates a wider truth—that crises do not only destroy wealth, they redistribute power. In Japan, the victims of collapse were not merely farmers or merchants but the very idea of civilian government itself.

The themes ahead speak to enduring dilemmas. How do societies respond when global trade fails them? What happens when national identity becomes entwined with economic rescue? And why do some nations reform internally while others turn outward with clenched fists? By following Japan's path from silk markets to the conquest of Manchuria, we glimpse not only the roots of its imperial expansion but also a universal warning: when democratic institutions falter under economic strain, the march of the soldier can appear, to many, as the march of salvation.

The story that unfolds here is one of choices made under duress, of markets that failed and of generals who filled the void. It is a narrative of how crisis blurred into conquest, and how a nation convinced itself that empire was the price of survival. The consequences, for Asia and the world, would be nothing less than catastrophic.

Export Collapse and Political Crisis

In 1929, a farmer in Nagano Prefecture bundled up his daughter and sold her to a silk-broker in Tokyo. She was fourteen, and her labour in the spinning mills would keep the family alive for another season. Scenes like this were repeated across rural Japan, where households depended on the export of raw silk to the United States. When the Depression shattered global markets, silk prices plummeted by two-thirds in a matter of months, and families found themselves stripped of livelihood and dignity. The collapse of an international commodity cascaded into a collapse of faith—not only in markets but in the civilian politicians who had tethered Japan's future to them.

The paradox was cruel. Japan had modernised with remarkable speed, weaving itself into the global economy as both an exporter of silk and textiles and an importer of vital raw materials. In the buoyant 1920s, this export engine symbolised the nation's ascent, a proof that it could prosper within the rules of global capitalism. Yet the very openness that had enabled growth became the Achilles' heel of the Japanese economy when the Depression struck. Unlike the United States, where internal markets offered some buffer, or Germany, which could lobby for debt relief, Japan was at the mercy of overseas demand. Its prosperity was contingent; its sovereignty, exposed.

The human costs were immediate and brutal. Rural Japan bore the deepest scars. Farmers, already pressed by debt, saw their incomes collapse by half between 1929 and 1931. With no social safety net, they sold children into factories or brothels, or abandoned land altogether. In the cities, unemployment swelled, bankruptcies multiplied, and hunger protests erupted. A generation that had been told democracy would deliver modern security now watched parliamentary politicians haggle over tariffs while the nation starved. The wounds were not only economic—they were moral, eroding confidence in the liberal experiment of the Taishō years.

Civilian leaders compounded the crisis with indecision. The government tried piecemeal interventions—currency deflation under Finance Minister Inoue Junnosuke, attempts at trade diversification—but these measures often deepened suffering rather than alleviated it. Deflation devastated indebted farmers, and austerity made credit scarcer. The sight of politicians clinging to orthodoxy while ordinary people endured misery fuelled the perception that civilian government was not merely ineffective but callous. Parliamentary democracy, still fragile after only a decade of universal male suffrage, seemed incapable of safeguarding the national interest.

The military capitalised on this disillusionment with ruthless skill. Army officers argued that Japan's dependence on volatile foreign markets was a betrayal of national sovereignty. They claimed only expansion into resource-rich territories could secure independence from the whims of capitalist cycles. The collapse of silk exports thus became not just an economic disaster but a political weapon. To the militarists, every suicide in the countryside and every closed factory in the cities was proof that Japan's destiny lay not in international trade but in empire.

The crisis illuminated a deeper philosophical divide: was prosperity to be secured through integration with global capitalism, or through autarky enforced by the sword? Civilian leaders clung to the former even as the evidence of its fragility mounted. The military promoted the latter as both practical and patriotic, a cure for economic dependency and an assertion of national pride. It was a stark choice between vulnerability and control, between parliamentary drift and decisive action. In that atmosphere of despair, radical certainty triumphed over hesitant moderation.

Yet the appeal of militarism was not merely strategic. It promised dignity to those who felt humiliated by dependency. It transformed economic victimhood into a narrative of national betrayal and redemption. The Depression was thus not only a financial crisis but a crisis of meaning: a society that had embraced global integration discovered it could be cast adrift by forces beyond its control. For many, the military's vision of seizing security through conquest seemed less reckless than trusting again in markets that had betrayed them.

The export collapse of 1929–31, then, was not an isolated economic event. It was the pivot on which Japan's politics turned from civilian rule to military ascendancy. Economic ruin discredited compromise, and in its place emerged a politics of absolutes. But the question remained unresolved: could conquest truly substitute for markets, or would the pursuit of autarky entangle Japan in conflicts far costlier than any trade crisis? The answer, as the decade unfolded, would shape the fate of Asia and the world.

Nationalism as an Economic Cure

In 1931, as Japanese troops marched into Manchuria, the operation was not described in Tokyo merely as a military manoeuvre. It was framed as a harvest. The barren, overpopulated islands of the home nation, where farmers sold daughters into factories and rice riots erupted with each poor crop, were said to be taking possession of a fertile frontier. Conquest was presented not as aggression but as relief, a national welfare policy with bayonets. In speeches, pamphlets, and newspapers, the seizure of Manchuria was cast as the rational answer to scarcity: Japan's population was rising, its land constrained, its dependence on foreign imports intolerable. If the world of markets was closed or treacherous, the world of territory could be forcibly opened.

The paradox was stark. Expansionism was sold as an economic policy, a substitute for the reforms and redistributions that might have relieved hardship at home. Politicians and military leaders argued that national strength required secure access to resources—coal, iron, soya, land for settlement—and that these could not be guaranteed by trade agreements vulnerable to Western tariffs and boycotts. By annexing or dominating neighbouring territories, Japan could achieve *self-sufficiency*, or so the rhetoric promised. Scarcity, in this worldview, was not a problem of production or inequality but of national boundaries. The cure lay not in reforming capitalism but in transcending it through conquest.

This vision had roots in older anxieties. Since the late nineteenth century, Japanese elites had feared "resource poverty," warning that the nation's survival depended on expansion into Asia. The Depression intensified these fears. The collapse of silk exports left millions destitute, and the Western powers, instead of offering relief, raised barriers. American tariffs on Japanese textiles and British imperial preference in Asian markets looked to many like a strangulation of Japan's future. Militarist ideologues took these developments as proof that international capitalism was a hostile system designed to keep Japan subordinate. Nationalism thus fused with economics: to resist humiliation and to secure prosperity were one and the same.

The rhetoric was powerfully persuasive because it transmuted humiliation into pride. Instead of being beggars at the tables of the Western powers, Japanese citizens were told they were pioneers carving out destiny. The army's capture of Manchurian mines and railways was depicted as the foundation of a new prosperity, one insulated from global downturns. School textbooks spoke of the "lifeline" that Manchuria provided; newspapers extolled the promise of migration and industrial wealth. Economic pain at home was reimagined as sacrifice for a national rebirth.

Yet this "cure" was built on illusions and coercion. The benefits of conquest flowed disproportionately to industrial conglomerates and the military establishment, while ordinary farmers and workers continued to endure hardship. Colonised populations, meanwhile, bore the costs in forced labour, land seizures, and political repression. To call expansion an economic remedy was to hide the reality that Japan's stability was purchased through violence inflicted elsewhere. The story was one of redistribution, not of abundance: hunger and unemployment in the home islands were eased at the expense of Chinese peasants displaced by Japanese settlement and labourers conscripted into mines and factories.

There was also an intellectual allure to the doctrine. For many Japanese thinkers, nationalism promised an escape from the contradictions of liberal capitalism. If markets were unpredictable, states could impose order; if democracy was weak, the nation's will could be asserted through hierarchy and discipline. Expansionism gave concrete form to this philosophy. It was not only a programme of military aggression but a narrative of meaning, an answer to the despair of a society that felt excluded from global prosperity.

By invading Manchuria and later moving deeper into China, Japan was not merely extending territory—it was dramatising the claim that strength, not dependence, was the path to survival.

Contradictions, however, gnawed at the project. Far from achieving true autarky, the empire remained reliant on imports of oil, rubber, and other strategic materials. The more Japan expanded, the more its appetite grew, pulling it into a spiral of conquests that outpaced its ability to consolidate gains. At home, too, militarist economic nationalism displaced political debate. Parliamentary politics, with their messy compromises, seemed decadent beside the clarity of the "national mission." The language of scarcity and cure became the language of inevitability: only through expansion could Japan endure.

The appeal of this narrative extended beyond economics. It promised dignity, unity, and purpose at a time when liberal institutions looked incapable of delivering them. Where the civilian government seemed paralysed, the army offered direction. Where markets seemed unreliable, conquest promised certainty. Nationalism thus became a salve for both stomachs and souls. But beneath the confidence of this economic cure lay a deeper sickness: a refusal to imagine solutions that did not involve domination.

The militarists' answer to scarcity was intoxicating because it simplified the world. Instead of confronting questions of inequality, land reform, or industrial overproduction, it externalised the crisis. The enemy was not within but without; salvation lay not in self-critique but in conquest. It was a story that relieved anxiety even as it stoked aggression. And it left open a haunting question: if expansionism could be justified as an economic cure once, what limits could ever restrain it?

The Manchurian Gambit

On the night of 18 September 1931, a small explosion tore up a section of railway track outside the Chinese city of Mukden. The blast caused minimal damage, scarcely enough to halt a train. Yet within hours, Japanese officers stationed nearby declared Chinese sabotage and unleashed a full-scale invasion of Manchuria. What began as a staged incident engineered by the Kwantung Army spiralled into one of the most consequential gambles of the interwar years. In the eyes of Tokyo's civilian leaders, the move was reckless; in the rhetoric of the army, it was destiny. Behind the theatrics lay a deeper reality: economic desperation was driving a major power to convert its insecurity into territorial conquest.

The Mukden Incident, as it came to be known, symbolised the fragility of Japan's democracy and the potency of militarist logic in a time of crisis. By 1931, the collapse of silk exports had devastated rural Japan, leaving farmers unable to pay taxes and forcing families to sell daughters into urban labour or prostitution. Industrialists complained of shuttered factories, while waves of unemployed men filled the streets. International trade, once the engine of Japan's modernisation, appeared hostile and unreliable as Western powers turned inward behind tariffs and imperial preference. In this climate, the army's seizure of Manchuria was framed as an economic lifeline—land for settlement, coal and iron for industry, soya for food and livestock feed. What could not be secured through commerce, Japan would now seize through force.

The logic was not uniquely Japanese. Across the world in the early 1930s, nations sought security in protectionism, imperial preference, or radical ideologies. But the Manchurian case was distinctive in its audacity. Unlike Britain or the United States, which turned to tariffs, Japan used the bayonet as a trade policy. Expansion into Manchuria was cast as the remedy to structural weakness: a vast, resource-rich territory that could deliver self-sufficiency and insulate Japan from the storms of global capitalism. For military leaders, this was not aggression but a necessary adaptation to international betrayal.

The gamble paid immediate dividends at home. The conquest was rapid and largely unopposed by Chinese forces, and the establishment of the puppet state of Manchukuo in 1932 was celebrated as a national triumph. Newspapers extolled it as proof of Japan's resilience and superiority; schoolchildren were taught to view Manchuria as their "lifeline." For millions facing hunger, the narrative of new land and resources was intoxicating. The boldness of the army contrasted sharply with the timidity of civilian politicians, who appeared paralysed in the face of economic collapse. In a society searching for certainty, the military's decisiveness was magnetic.

Yet the gambit also exposed profound contradictions. Internationally, it isolated Japan. The League of Nations condemned the invasion, but its inability to act decisively only deepened Tokyo's disdain for the international order. Withdrawal from the League in 1933 marked a rupture: Japan had chosen the path of unilateral conquest over cooperative diplomacy. Economically, too, Manchuria was no simple solution. While rich in resources, the costs of occupation and development far outstripped immediate gains. Rather than easing Japan's crisis, the conquest tied the nation to a costly imperial project that demanded ever more military spending and expansion to be justified.

The deeper significance of the Manchurian Gambit lies in its fusion of economics and geopolitics. Scarcity was transformed into a rationale for aggression; insecurity was reimagined as opportunity. The Mukden Incident was more than a pretext—it was a theatre in which Japan dramatised a new worldview: that national survival could no longer depend on markets or diplomacy, but only on force. The gambit thus represented not just a territorial conquest but a psychological turning point, eroding the legitimacy of parliamentary governance and embedding the military as the nation's vanguard.

The story also illuminates a broader truth about crisis politics. When economic collapse erodes faith in existing systems, radical actors gain power by offering certainty. Japan's militarists offered not prosperity in the liberal sense but security through conquest, a vision that redefined economic health as territorial control. It was a seductive idea, precisely because it was simple: instead of grappling with inequality, inefficiency, or reform, Japan could reach for the resources of others.

But gambles are, by nature, unstable. The seizure of Manchuria bought temporary acclaim but set Japan on a trajectory of escalating commitments it could not easily escape. Each conquest created the need for another, each occupation deepened hostility abroad and dependence at home. What began as a response to the Depression soon became a habit of expansion that propelled Japan into total war.

The Manchurian Gambit thus stands as both a triumph and a trap. It reveals how economic desperation, when filtered through nationalist ideology and militarist ambition, can transmute into aggressive geopolitics. It also leaves us with a sobering question: when scarcity is weaponised as justification for expansion, what forces remain to halt the momentum of conquest once it begins?

Civilian Retreat, Military Advance

In May 1932, a group of young naval officers stormed the streets of Tokyo, assassinating Prime Minister Inukai Tsuyoshi in his home. Their bullets ended the life of Japan's last truly independent civilian leader of the pre-war era. What shocked the nation was not only the act itself, but the muted response that followed. Courts handed down lenient sentences; crowds gathered outside prisons to cheer the perpetrators. Democracy had been attacked in broad daylight—and the public, weary of hardship and disillusioned with politicians, seemed less outraged than resigned.

The assassination was not an isolated outrage but the culmination of a long erosion of parliamentary authority under the weight of the Great Depression. In the 1920s, Japan had briefly appeared to be following a constitutionalist path. Parties competed for office, and cabinets relied on parliamentary majorities. Yet this fragile experiment proved ill-suited to a system where the military was constitutionally autonomous and economic shocks were devastating. When exports collapsed and rural communities starved, civilian governments faltered in their attempts to act decisively. Military leaders, presenting themselves as men of action, stepped into the vacuum.

The fragility of Japan's democracy was partly institutional. The Meiji Constitution of 1889 enshrined the armed forces' direct line to the emperor, ensuring that neither parliament nor cabinet could restrain generals and admirals. This design, initially intended as a safeguard against partisan meddling, became a loophole through which the military steadily expanded influence. In practice, party cabinets needed military ministers to govern, yet the services could refuse to appoint them, effectively paralysing governments. As economic pressures mounted in the 1930s, this imbalance was exploited with ruthless efficiency.

Civilian politicians did little to inspire confidence. Prime Ministers of the Depression era cycled through office rapidly, unable to articulate a coherent programme for recovery. Attempts to balance budgets, stabilise the yen, and satisfy international creditors seemed out of touch with the desperation of ordinary citizens. Farmers sold daughters to brothels; labourers queued at soup kitchens; disillusionment turned to anger. Against this backdrop, the military's calls for national renewal through expansion and sacrifice resonated with audiences who saw little to lose.

The contrast between words and deeds proved decisive. Civilian cabinets talked of reform but wavered when faced with entrenched interests and international constraints. By contrast, the Kwantung Army's unauthorised seizure of Manchuria in 1931, though illegal, was celebrated as a bold solution to economic scarcity. Civilian leaders condemned the action, yet lacked the authority to reverse it. Their impotence made them appear weak, while the military reaped prestige. Each such episode chipped away at the legitimacy of parliamentary governance, until assassination and intimidation became tools of routine politics.

The erosion of democratic norms was not merely structural; it was cultural. A generation of young officers, radicalised by hardship in the countryside and emboldened by nationalist ideologues, embraced violence as political expression. They denounced party politicians as corrupt, beholden to business cliques and foreign powers. When they struck against civilian leaders, they framed their actions not as rebellion but as purification—a cleansing of the nation's body politic. That many ordinary citizens sympathised with this rhetoric reflected how far faith in parliamentary democracy had collapsed.

Japan's story in the 1930s demonstrates how economic crisis can corrode institutions from within. Democracy does not always fall to a single coup; sometimes it withers through gradual delegitimation. When elected leaders cannot deliver stability, when institutions appear incapable of decisive action, the allure of men in uniform grows. The military promises order, clarity, and sacrifice, qualities that can seem attractive when civilian politics looks compromised and hesitant. The Depression amplified these dynamics, turning Japan's fragile parliamentary experiment into an object of derision.

What makes this trajectory striking is how familiar it feels. The Japanese public did not initially reject democracy; rather, many became indifferent to its erosion. Each concession to the military seemed temporary, each retreat justified by necessity, until the line between expediency and surrender blurred. Civilian elites who hoped to outmanoeuvre or appease the military instead legitimised it further. By the mid-1930s, Japan's parliamentary institutions still existed on paper but had lost their essence: the ability to check power, to reflect popular will, to shape national direction.

The collapse of civilian rule in Japan was not inevitable, yet it unfolded with the quiet inevitability of a tide. It shows how quickly democratic systems can be hollowed out when legitimacy drains away, and how easily military actors can step forward when institutions stumble. It raises a sobering question that lingers beyond its time: when hardship deepens and faith in politics falters, what prevents citizens from trading democracy for discipline, uncertainty for the iron promise of command?

The Road Toward Empire

In 1937, smoke rose over Shanghai as Japanese troops advanced into the city, transforming commercial districts into battlegrounds. Newspapers across the world carried images of the devastation, evidence that a once peripheral island nation had now set itself on a collision course with Asia and beyond. To many observers, the assault on China was shocking in scale but unsurprising in trajectory. Japan's plunge into empire was not the product of sudden ambition; it was the culmination of years in which domestic crisis had been displaced outward, turned into an ideology of conquest.

The paradox of Japan in the 1930s was stark. At the very moment when other nations were experimenting with welfare reforms, currency stabilisation, and industrial restructuring, Japan's response to the Depression was to look abroad rather than within. Political paralysis at home, compounded by the military's ascendancy, closed the door on meaningful reform. Instead of confronting structural inequalities or investing in social stability, leaders redefined scarcity as a call for expansion. Hunger, unemployment, and industrial dependence were recast as justifications for seizing land and resources from neighbours.

The seizure of Manchuria in 1931 was the pivot. What had begun as a unilateral act by rogue officers became national policy when Tokyo, rather than disciplining the perpetrators, embraced their fait accompli. Manchuria's mines, railways, and agricultural lands were presented as a lifeline—a "lifeboat" economy that would insulate Japan from global volatility. Yet Manchuria was not only about resources. It was a demonstration that aggressive action abroad could rally public support in ways no domestic measure could. The occupation boosted national pride, lent the military political legitimacy, and created a template for further expansion.

Each crisis thereafter was met with the same externalising reflex. When silk exports, the backbone of rural income, collapsed, politicians did not propose agricultural subsidies or land reforms; they looked to continental markets. When industrialists feared shortages of coal, iron, and oil, the solution was not technological innovation but territorial annexation. Expansion became less a strategy than an instinct, a means of reconciling domestic failure with the illusion of forward movement. The Great Depression had taught Japan's leaders a perverse lesson: empire could stand in for reform.

The costs of this logic became apparent quickly. Occupying Manchuria strained finances and international credibility. The League of Nations condemned Japan's aggression, but instead of retreating, Tokyo walked out of the organisation altogether in 1933. Isolation did not deter expansion; it deepened the conviction that Japan could rely only on itself, even if that meant dismantling the global order that had once integrated its economy. Autarky, militarised industry, and conquest became interwoven threads of a single national project.

Domestically, the road toward empire silenced alternative paths. Civilian politicians who had once advocated cautious diplomacy were marginalised or assassinated. Journalists and intellectuals who questioned expansion were censored. The military increasingly controlled budgets, education, and foreign policy, weaving narratives of national destiny into daily life. Democracy did not simply collapse—it was crowded out by a mobilisation that declared dissent unpatriotic and reform unmanly. The choice presented to citizens was stark: follow the empire's march or be cast aside as an obstacle to national survival.

This trajectory revealed a broader truth about the relationship between economics and geopolitics. For Japan, the Depression was not just a financial calamity but a psychological one, shaking confidence in both global trade and domestic politics. Expansion offered certainty, however brutal. By seizing resources, leaders promised to master scarcity; by projecting power, they reassured citizens of purpose. Yet such certainty came at the expense of stability. Every conquest required the next, each advance creating new vulnerabilities that could only be resolved by further aggression.

The invasion of China in 1937 was, in this sense, not an aberration but an inevitability. Having framed empire as the solution to crisis, Japan had no mechanism for restraint. The war that followed was devastating not only to China but to Japan itself, locking the nation into a path of overreach and confrontation with Western powers. The empire built as an answer to scarcity soon produced scarcity on a scale greater than any Depression-era crisis.

Japan's road toward empire underscores the dangers of externalising domestic problems. When societies choose conquest over reform, when they equate stability with expansion rather than compromise, they create conditions where war becomes the default solution to economic malaise. The Depression may have triggered this turn, but it was the failure to address internal fractures—social, political, and institutional—that made aggression seem inevitable.

The story leaves us with a question that still resonates. In times of profound economic insecurity, what determines whether nations look inward to rebuild or outward to seize? The answer is rarely obvious in the moment. Yet the Japanese case warns that when leaders cloak expansion in the language of necessity, when empire becomes the surrogate for reform, the road they build does not lead to stability but to catastrophe.

Chapter 7

Britain: The Cracks in Empire

On a foggy morning in September 1931, clerks rushed to the Bank of England carrying bags of gold sovereigns, hurriedly shipped abroad as nervous investors abandoned sterling. Within days, Britain—the country that had once been the unquestioned arbiter of the global financial system—was forced off the gold standard. The move was pragmatic, even inevitable, but its symbolism was devastating. A nation that had built its power on the stability of its currency now found itself conceding that the rules it had written for the world economy no longer worked. The cracks in empire were no longer hidden in colonial outposts; they had reached the very heart of London's financial district.

The paradox was sharp. Britain had once championed free trade as both ideology and imperial glue, confident that its industries, its fleets, and its credit would guarantee prosperity. Yet by the early 1930s, the reality was reversed: global trade had collapsed, the pound was under siege, and vast swathes of northern England stood idle. In mining towns across Durham and shipyards along the Clyde, unemployment was not a statistic but a way of life, forcing families to queue for meagre benefits while local economies atrophied. For millions, the Depression was not about balance sheets in the City but about whether bread could be put on the table.

The dissonance between orthodoxy and reality defined Britain's response. Leaders clung to principles of fiscal rectitude and global openness long after conditions demanded bold departure. When they did act—most notably by abandoning gold—it was under duress, framed as a reluctant necessity rather than a strategic reimagining. The coalition National Government that followed embodied this mindset. Formed in 1931, it presented itself as a unity measure to stabilise the nation but in practice became a mechanism for preserving elite consensus. Policy innovation was scarce; austerity, retrenchment, and political containment defined its legacy. It was less a government of renewal than a committee of national triage.

Yet Britain was not without options, nor was it passive. Facing industrial decline at home, it turned ever more heavily to its empire. The Ottawa Agreements of 1932 institutionalised imperial preference, constructing a protective economic bloc at a moment when global liberalism was collapsing. This offered short-term relief but carried long-term risks. By privileging colonial markets, Britain entrenched dependencies and sowed resentment, particularly among dominions that had begun to imagine economic sovereignty. The empire that was supposed to be Britain's cushion became instead a fragile scaffold, masking decline while foreshadowing future fractures.

This chapter examines Britain at a moment when the Depression exposed the limits of its imperial model. It follows the story from the collapse of free trade orthodoxy to the end of the gold standard, from unemployment in the industrial north to the rise of a National Government that confused stability with stagnation. It also considers how the empire—touted as salvation—became both a crutch and a constraint. At its heart lies a question that still resonates: what happens when a world power discovers that the tools that once secured dominance now bind it to decline?

The cracks that opened in the 1930s did not immediately destroy Britain's empire. But they revealed how fragile its foundations had become, and how economic crisis could ripple into questions of legitimacy, governance, and identity. The struggle to preserve order amid breakdown is a story not only of Britain in the Depression but of any society confronting the limits of its power. The question is not whether cracks appear, but how long they can be papered over before the structure shifts irrevocably.

The Collapse of Free Trade Orthodoxy

In 1932, delegates gathered in Ottawa to draft agreements that would fundamentally reshape Britain's trading relationships. For a nation that had long styled itself as the high priest of free trade, the very setting was symbolic: a conference in a dominion capital, not Westminster or the City of London, where new rules were to be written. Imperial preference, once derided as protectionist heresy, was now tabled as lifeline. To grasp the gravity of this turn, one must remember that for decades free trade was not simply an economic doctrine in Britain—it was a moral creed, a yardstick by which civilisation itself was measured. That it collapsed under Depression pressure tells us less about policy than about how ideology, once a source of pride, became a straitjacket in crisis.

The paradox is striking. Britain had built its nineteenth-century dominance on an unflinching belief that dismantling tariffs would guarantee prosperity. The repeal of the Corn Laws in 1846 was more than a trade policy shift; it was a declaration of national identity, a commitment to openness in exchange for cheaper food and expanded markets. By the eve of the First World War, free trade was so entrenched that it seemed beyond political contestation. Its defenders claimed it upheld peace, ensured efficiency, and distinguished Britain from the protectionist instincts of rivals like Germany and the United States. To abandon it, they argued, would be to betray the very soul of liberal Britain.

Yet the Great Depression struck at the heart of these assumptions. As world trade contracted—falling by nearly two-thirds between 1929 and 1933—Britain's reliance on overseas markets turned from asset to liability. Exports that had once sustained shipyards, steelworks, and textile mills shrank dramatically. By 1931, British exports had fallen by over 30 per cent, devastating industrial regions in the North and Scotland. What had been celebrated as openness now looked like exposure. The rules of the liberal game had changed, but Britain's political class hesitated, paralysed by the weight of tradition.

This hesitation was not simply a matter of economics; it reflected a deeper clash between ideology and reality. Free trade orthodoxy insisted that markets would self-correct, that Britain's financial supremacy and sterling's role as a global currency would restore equilibrium. To question this was to question decades of national self-belief. Yet unemployment queues lengthened, tax revenues collapsed, and political legitimacy wavered. Policymakers were trapped in a bind: to abandon free trade would risk undermining Britain's global prestige; to cling to it threatened domestic ruin.

The debates within Cabinet and among economists of the time illustrate the intensity of the struggle. Figures like Winston Churchill, who had controversially returned Britain to the gold standard at an overvalued rate in 1925, remained wedded to the orthodoxy that credibility demanded sacrifice. Critics, including John Maynard Keynes, argued that dogmatic adherence to free trade and gold was strangling recovery, likening Britain to a patient being bled dry by outdated medicine. Keynes's call for managed trade and active state intervention directly challenged the Victorian inheritance. The intellectual battle was as fierce as the political one, revealing how hard it is for societies to abandon frameworks that have defined them.

Eventually, pragmatism forced Britain's hand. The sterling crisis of 1931 drove the country off the gold standard, while the Ottawa Agreements of 1932 entrenched a new system of imperial preference. These were not triumphant reforms but reluctant retreats. Rather than announcing a bold new model, policymakers cloaked their decisions in the language of necessity, as if betraying free trade could only be justified under duress. The shift, therefore, carried an air of defeat rather than renewal, an acknowledgment that the empire's economic core could no longer sustain itself under the old rules.

The social consequences of this collapse were profound. In towns like Jarrow, Middlesbrough, and Merthyr Tydfil, where industries depended on global markets, the orthodoxy of free trade translated into closed factories and breadlines. Ordinary citizens paid the price for elites' refusal to adapt. This disconnect between ideology and lived reality deepened cynicism about parliamentary politics and fuelled support for radical alternatives, from communism to Oswald Mosley's British Union of Fascists. Free trade, once hailed as a bulwark of liberal democracy, was increasingly seen as the indulgence of out-of-touch elites.

At the same time, imperial preference raised its own dilemmas. By privileging trade within the empire, Britain attempted to insulate itself from global turbulence. Yet this reliance carried a double edge: it bound the dominions more tightly to Britain but also revealed how dependent the metropole had become on colonial markets. For countries like Canada and Australia, the arrangement fostered resentment, as imperial economics appeared to subordinate their own aspirations for independence. Thus, what seemed a cure for Britain's immediate crisis planted seeds of long-term fracture within the empire itself.

The collapse of free trade orthodoxy highlights a broader truth: when ideology becomes identity, policy cannot easily adapt to reality. Britain's leaders faced a Depression that demanded flexibility, yet they were constrained by doctrines that had once delivered supremacy. Theirs was not simply a failure of economics but of imagination. By clinging to free trade until crisis forced retreat, they revealed how power is lost—not in dramatic defeats, but in the slow erosion of the ability to change.

The tension remains resonant. In every era, societies must ask whether cherished principles are sustaining or shackling them. Britain's ordeal in the 1930s illustrates the danger of confusing doctrine with destiny, of assuming that rules once written can endure forever. As the Depression showed, when the world shifts, even empires must decide whether to bend or risk breaking. And the question that lingered after Ottawa was whether Britain's compromise had preserved strength—or merely disguised decline.

Sterling Crisis and the End of Gold

On 21 September 1931, the British government announced that sterling would no longer be convertible into gold at a fixed rate. The statement was brief, couched in the language of necessity, but its implications were seismic. For decades, the gold standard had underpinned Britain's claim to global financial leadership. London's bankers, traders, and policymakers had seen it not merely as a mechanism of exchange but as the very architecture of credibility. To abandon it was unthinkable—until it became unavoidable. That moment of capitulation marked both a pragmatic response to acute crisis and a symbolic admission that the foundations of empire's financial dominance were crumbling.

The paradox was stark. The gold standard had been championed as the guarantor of stability, a self-imposed discipline that prevented reckless spending and inflation. For Britain, whose imperial reach rested on both military power and financial prestige, adherence to gold was not only economic orthodoxy but a badge of honour. Sterling's role as a reserve currency, trusted across continents, rested on the assurance that it could always be exchanged for gold at a fixed value. To leave the standard was to risk reputational collapse—yet by 1931, remaining on it threatened national ruin.

The immediate context was one of cascading pressures. The Great Depression had already battered Britain's export industries, driving unemployment to nearly three million. The government, committed to defending the pound's parity, imposed austerity measures—cutting public wages and benefits—to reassure international markets. Instead of restoring confidence, these measures deepened domestic anger. The final trigger came with the Invergordon Mutiny of September 1931, when Royal Navy sailors, incensed by pay cuts, refused orders. The sight of rebellion within the armed forces sent shockwaves through markets. Investors, fearing instability, launched a run on sterling, draining Britain's gold reserves at an alarming pace. Within days, the Treasury could no longer defend the pound. The gold standard was sacrificed, not as a planned reform but as an emergency retreat.

To contemporaries, the decision carried immense psychological weight. For some, it was liberation: freed from the constraints of gold, Britain could pursue policies tailored to domestic recovery, including cheaper credit and a managed exchange rate. Indeed, the pound's depreciation boosted exports and helped stabilise employment. Yet for others, the break signalled humiliation. A country that had once dictated the rules of global finance was now bending to necessity. The gold standard had been not just a policy but a metaphor for Britain's claim to order and discipline. Its collapse hinted at deeper fragility: if London could no longer uphold monetary orthodoxy, what else in the imperial system might give way?

The reactions abroad underscored this symbolism. France, still committed to gold, viewed Britain's decision as betrayal. The United States, itself reeling from bank failures, interpreted it as a warning that no currency was unassailable. Within the empire, the move deepened dependence, as dominions linked their currencies more closely to sterling in its new, less exalted form. In practical terms, Britain remained a financial power; the City of London continued to channel vast flows of capital. But the aura of unchallengeable supremacy was gone. The sterling crisis had revealed that the empire's financial edifice, like its political one, was subject to erosion.

The intellectual fallout was equally significant. Economists who had long warned against the rigidity of gold, Keynes foremost among them, saw vindication. He argued that clinging to the standard in the face of Depression had inflicted needless suffering, and that flexibility—not dogma—was the true path to resilience. Yet even Keynes recognised that abandoning gold did not erase the deeper challenge: Britain's relative economic decline compared with the United States and Germany. The end of gold was less a new beginning than an admission that the old order could no longer be sustained.

At the human level, the sterling crisis reflected the disjuncture between abstract financial orthodoxy and lived experience. For the unemployed shipbuilder in Glasgow or the miner in South Wales, gold was a remote concern. What mattered was the reality of hunger, eviction, and despair. The government's commitment to defending the pound at all costs seemed, to many, proof that elites valued international credibility over domestic survival. When the policy collapsed, it underscored a bitter truth: sacrifices demanded in the name of stability had been in vain. The crisis thus not only reshaped economic policy but also widened the gap of trust between rulers and ruled.

Looking back, the decision to leave gold appears both inevitable and transformative. It allowed Britain to stabilise more quickly than many other nations, proving that orthodoxy can become an obstacle rather than a solution. But the deeper symbolism cannot be ignored. The end of gold marked the waning of Britain's role as unquestioned financial arbiter of the world. Sterling would remain important, but never again would it embody the same aura of immutable stability. The empire had crossed an invisible threshold: it could still adapt, but it could no longer dictate.

The sterling crisis forces us to confront a perennial question: when do principles sustain strength, and when do they become chains that drag nations down? Britain's reluctant abandonment of the gold standard reveals the fragility of even the most entrenched systems. In 1931, the empire preserved itself by betraying its own creed. Whether that act represented resilience or decline remained contested then—and remains so now.

Unemployment in the North

In November 1930, a journalist visiting Jarrow described the scene as "streets of silent men." The shipyards lay dormant, the furnaces cold, and the pavements filled with men who had once built the great vessels of empire but now stood idle, staring at nothing in particular. Children played with empty tins in alleyways while their mothers queued at relief offices for meagre allowances. Jarrow was not an isolated case. Across Britain's industrial North—from the Durham coalfields to the textile towns of Lancashire—the collapse of staple industries transformed communities into landscapes of despair. Here, the Great Depression was not an abstract matter of falling trade balances; it was the lived reality of hunger, humiliation, and wasted skill.

The paradox was acute. These towns had once been the beating heart of Britain's industrial might, places that symbolised modernity and resilience. Coal, steel, and textiles had fuelled both the nation's prosperity and its imperial reach. Yet, as world trade contracted, it was precisely these export-driven industries that proved most vulnerable. By the early 1930s, unemployment in mining regions hovered between 40 and 70 per cent. Entire towns were hollowed out. The same communities that had underpinned Britain's power now became symbols of its decline.

Take the example of South Wales, where coal exports had once sustained bustling valleys. By 1932, demand had collapsed so dramatically that pits closed in succession, leaving thousands of miners without work. Relief payments barely covered subsistence, and the stigma of dependency weighed heavily on men whose identities were bound to labour and solidarity. In Durham, similar patterns unfolded. Villages built around a single colliery saw their entire economic lifeblood severed when the pit shut down. The result was not only material poverty but also social unravelling: pawn shops thrived, birth rates fell, and malnutrition became widespread.

The psychological toll cannot be overstated. In mining and shipbuilding communities, work was more than wages; it was the foundation of dignity, masculinity, and belonging. The sudden and prolonged absence of work eroded these pillars. Men described feeling "buried alive," stripped of purpose. Families lived in constant tension, with domestic roles upended by enforced idleness. Unemployment was thus not simply an economic statistic but a profound assault on identity and social cohesion.

From this dislocation arose radical alternatives. Disillusionment with the parliamentary system ran deep in the North, where many believed London's politicians neither understood nor cared about their plight. The Communist Party, though small nationally, gained traction in depressed areas by organising hunger marches and framing unemployment as proof of capitalism's failure. The National Unemployed Workers' Movement orchestrated demonstrations that brought thousands into the streets, demanding jobs or relief. The 1936 Jarrow Crusade, in which 200 men marched 300 miles to London to demand work, encapsulated both the desperation and the determination of these communities.

Yet the appeal of radicalism was not confined to the left. Some disillusioned workers turned instead towards right-wing movements, seduced by promises of national renewal and disdain for a political class seen as corrupt and ineffectual. The British Union of Fascists, led by Oswald Mosley, found pockets of support in the North, particularly where bitterness and anger outweighed hope. Unemployment thus became a crucible of political experimentation, a testing ground for ideologies that sought to fill the void left by economic collapse.

At the same time, the resilience of these communities was remarkable. Mutual aid societies, chapels, and trade unions provided both practical relief and emotional solidarity. Soup kitchens and co-operatives sprang up, ensuring survival even in the harshest conditions. Cultural life persisted—miners wrote poetry, choirs performed, football clubs rallied crowds. In the face of abandonment, people found ways to assert dignity and collective identity. This endurance complicates any simplistic narrative of despair.

Philosophically, the North's experience raises enduring questions about the relationship between work, identity, and democracy. If entire regions are left idle, how long can faith in democratic institutions survive? What happens when communities built on productive labour are consigned to redundancy by global forces beyond their control? These questions, posed in the 1930s, remain strikingly relevant in an age of deindustrialisation and automation.

The case studies of Jarrow, South Wales, and Durham reveal a truth that statistics alone cannot capture: unemployment was both an economic crisis and a social fracture. The silence of idle streets was the sound of political legitimacy ebbing away. The radical alternatives that sprouted in its place were not born of ideology alone but of lived despair and the search for meaning in conditions of abandonment.

Britain's rulers managed to contain these pressures without the collapse of parliamentary democracy, unlike in parts of Europe. Yet containment did not equal resolution. The unemployment of the North left scars that shaped political memory for decades, fuelling distrust of elites and a yearning for more responsive governance. The silence of Jarrow's streets continues to echo, reminding us that economic collapse is never just about markets—it is about people, their hopes, and the systems they come to believe in or reject.

And so the question lingers: when the very communities that built a nation are left to wither, what form of politics—radical, authoritarian, or democratic—will step forward to claim their allegiance?

The Rise of the National Government

On a grey August morning in 1931, Ramsay MacDonald walked through the gates of Buckingham Palace to seek the King's support. He was not arriving to defend his Labour government but to preside over its dismantling. Within days, MacDonald—once a symbol of working-class politics—was leading a coalition dominated by Conservatives. To his supporters, it was betrayal; to his critics on the right, a triumph. To both, it symbolised the primacy of "stability" over the promises of reform. The National Government was born not out of vision but out of crisis management, a desperate contrivance designed to reassure markets, calm creditors, and maintain the status quo.

The paradox was glaring. Britain, facing mass unemployment, collapsing trade, and the crumbling of its financial orthodoxy, needed bold innovation. Yet the solution that emerged was a coalition defined by caution, where innovation was treated less as necessity than as risk. It was a government of national unity in name but of conservative instincts in practice. Its legitimacy rested not on solving the Depression but on containing it—proving once more that in moments of profound instability, political elites often prefer *managing decline* to imagining alternatives.

The immediate trigger was the sterling crisis of summer 1931. As international investors lost faith in Britain's ability to defend the pound and balance its budget, capital fled, foreign reserves dwindled, and pressure mounted for drastic cuts. The Labour government split over demands to reduce unemployment benefits. MacDonald and a handful of allies accepted the logic of austerity; most of his party did not. Faced with stalemate, the King and leading Conservatives engineered a coalition, installing MacDonald as figurehead but ceding the machinery of policy to Conservative dominance. The irony was brutal: a Labour prime minister presided over measures that betrayed his party's core supporters.

The National Government's hallmark was restraint disguised as necessity. It slashed public spending, cut unemployment benefits by 10 per cent, and reduced public-sector pay. These measures appeased financial markets but inflicted acute pain on the very communities already decimated by joblessness. Shipyard workers in Jarrow, coal miners in South Wales, and textile labourers in Lancashire bore the brunt of policies framed as essential for national survival. For them, the "national" in National Government was a bitter misnomer; unity was secured at their expense.

The coalition's claim to authority rested on the narrative of inevitability. Leaders presented their measures as unavoidable, dictated by economic circumstance rather than political choice. In doing so, they narrowed the horizon of democratic possibility. Alternative solutions—such as large-scale public works, state-led industrial investment, or more radical currency reform—were dismissed as reckless experiments. Britain's rulers invoked stability as both shield and weapon, conflating elite consensus with national interest. The Depression, in this telling, required discipline rather than imagination.

Philosophically, this raises an enduring tension: in times of crisis, does democracy serve as a vehicle for bold transformation or as a mechanism for entrenching caution? The National Government leaned firmly towards the latter. By broadening its base through coalition, it insulated itself from meaningful opposition, transforming politics into the art of managerial compromise. Yet this broadness masked fragility. It was unity not forged by common vision but by fear of collapse—an alliance against alternatives, rather than for solutions.

The electoral landslide of 1931, in which the National Government won overwhelming support, complicates the picture. Many Britons, frightened by economic turmoil and reassured by the appeal to unity, endorsed the coalition. The sheer scale of victory suggested legitimacy. Yet the results also revealed how fear can be mobilised to hollow out meaningful choice. Voters were offered a stark dichotomy: stability with the coalition, or chaos with its opponents. Faced with this framing, the electorate ratified caution, though not necessarily conviction.

For those in the industrial North and Wales, the coalition's policies deepened alienation. Relief cuts aggravated hardship, and the sense of betrayal festered. Parliamentary politics seemed remote, unresponsive, even complicit in suffering. This disconnect between elite consensus and popular experience proved fertile ground for disillusionment. While Britain did not collapse into authoritarianism, as some European states did, the gap between rulers and ruled widened. The stability preserved at Westminster came at the price of faith in its capacity to deliver change.

One might argue that the National Government did achieve a measure of pragmatic success. By leaving the gold standard in September 1931 and later adopting tariffs, it allowed for modest recovery. Yet even these shifts, though significant, were framed as reluctant necessities rather than deliberate innovation. The coalition never articulated a new economic vision; it survived by muddling through, anchored more in fear of rupture than in pursuit of renewal. Its endurance owed less to popular enthusiasm than to the absence of credible alternatives within the existing political framework.

The story of the National Government is therefore less about the particulars of 1931 than about the perennial instincts of political elites under duress. Faced with crisis, they coalesce, constrain, and consolidate. Innovation is delayed, often until the crisis deepens or external pressures force change. The coalition's very longevity—stretching through much of the 1930s—illustrates the resilience of managerial politics. But it also reveals its limits: by deferring reform, it ensured that deeper fractures remained unresolved, only to resurface with greater force later.

As we look back, the rise of the National Government invites a sobering reflection: when crisis strikes, is political stability always to be prized above imaginative reform? Britain's elites of 1931 answered emphatically in the affirmative. They preserved order, yes—but at the cost of perpetuating decline. And the unanswered question lingers still: when the next great crisis demands not merely management but transformation, will political leaders dare to choose differently?

Imperial Diversions

In the autumn of 1932, the streets of Ottawa bustled with delegates from across the British Empire. Politicians, bankers, and industrialists crowded into hotels and meeting halls to debate a simple but fateful question: could the empire save itself by closing ranks? The Ottawa Conference became the stage where Britain, humbled by the Depression and forced off the gold standard, sought solace not in innovation at home but in the embrace of its imperial family. Tariff walls rose where once free trade had been the empire's creed, and "imperial preference" was championed as both shield and salvation. What looked like economic pragmatism in the moment was, in fact, a diversion—a turning away from deeper structural reform and a bet that empire could buffer decline.

The paradox was stark. For decades Britain had preached the virtues of free trade as the foundation of its global strength. Now, with its exports collapsing and its financial pre-eminence shattered, it invoked the empire as a captive market and safety net. The very ideology that had justified British dominance—liberal, open, universalist—was abandoned for a narrower, more defensive vision. The rhetoric shifted from global leadership to imperial exclusivity. The Depression, in this sense, did not just shake Britain's economy; it fractured the intellectual scaffolding of its empire.

Yet the promise of imperial relief was always more fragile than its champions admitted. India, the jewel in the crown, was itself in crisis, its textile workers laid off, its farmers crushed by falling commodity prices. Colonial subjects were expected to consume more British goods and supply raw materials on favourable terms, even as they struggled with their own economic emergencies. The logic of "imperial preference" was extractive at its core: stability for Britain, sacrifice for the periphery. Behind the scenes, it deepened resentment among colonial populations, who saw clearly that their hardships were being harnessed to sustain a metropolis that could no longer sustain itself.

Case studies reveal the unevenness of this imperial strategy. In West Africa, Britain leaned heavily on cocoa and palm oil exports to bolster sterling reserves, even as producers faced ruinous price collapses. In the Caribbean, sugar planters were shielded by preferential tariffs, but workers endured wage cuts and mounting unrest. In India, nationalist leaders seized on the hypocrisy of imperial preference as evidence of Britain's exploitative intent. Far from solidifying loyalty, the Depression-era turn to empire seeded disillusionment and provided fuel for independence movements. The very mechanism that was meant to hold the empire together became an accelerant of its eventual dissolution.

Domestically, imperial diversions allowed Britain's leaders to avoid a reckoning with industrial decline at home. Shipbuilding, coal, and textiles—the core of northern industry—were not revived by imperial preference. Instead, policy choices entrenched regional disparities, leaving communities to languish while elites in London congratulated themselves on preserving sterling and balancing trade within the empire. The strategy bought breathing space but at the cost of entrenching structural weaknesses. Britain became increasingly dependent on imperial exploitation even as the foundations of its global authority eroded.

The imperial turn was also symbolic. It conveyed to the world that Britain, once the champion of global economic liberalism, now lacked the strength to defend its own orthodoxy. The United States and rising powers like Japan took note. Where Britain had once set the terms of global commerce, it now retreated into a defensive bloc. The language of "family" and "commonwealth" could not disguise the reality: Britain was signalling its diminished role on the world stage. Imperial preference was less a bold economic strategy than an admission of weakness, an attempt to patch the fabric of empire at the moment it was beginning to fray.

Philosophically, this moment invites reflection on the use of diversion as a political strategy. When faced with intractable domestic challenges, governments often look outward, redirecting attention and resources to external projects. For Britain in the 1930s, empire became both a lifeline and a distraction. It deferred the need for painful restructuring, postponed the acknowledgement of industrial obsolescence, and provided a stage for the rhetoric of unity. Yet diversions, however effective in the short term, rarely resolve the underlying problems. They buy time, but at a price.

The price here was high. By leaning on the empire for relief, Britain ensured that its economic policies became entangled with imperial tensions. Colonies were no longer simply passive sources of wealth; they were politically awakened societies, demanding fairness and, increasingly, independence. Every act of extraction, every tariff designed to privilege Britain, sharpened the contradictions of imperial rule. Economic expediency thus deepened political instability, sowing seeds that would later unravel not only the empire but also the global balance of power.

By the late 1930s, the illusion of imperial security was already cracking. Protectionist walls could not prevent the rise of American industrial dominance or the aggressive economic nationalism of Germany and Japan. Britain's reliance on empire, far from insulating it, left it vulnerable—tied to colonies that resented exploitation and exposed to competitors that had no interest in respecting imperial arrangements. What had been presented as a solution became a symptom: the empire was not a cure for Britain's decline but an emblem of it.

The story of imperial diversions therefore forces us to confront a deeper question: when nations cling to external props rather than confront internal weaknesses, do they postpone decline—or accelerate it? Britain's 1930s experiment with empire suggests the latter. Stability was purchased at the cost of legitimacy, and relief was fleeting. In the end, imperial preference did not secure Britain's dominance; it foreshadowed its end. And as the world hurtled towards war, the contradictions unleashed by this strategy would explode, reshaping not just Britain's empire but the global order itself.

Chapter 8

The Fragility of Democracies

In 1933, as Franklin D. Roosevelt raised his right hand to take the presidential oath, another leader just across the Atlantic was consolidating power through rallies, purges, and emergency decrees. Both men claimed to speak for democracy, both invoked renewal, and both emerged from nations crippled by economic ruin. Yet their paths diverged: one led his country into a cautious revival of democratic faith, the other into dictatorship and global war. This juxtaposition of Washington and Berlin is more than a historical curiosity; it is a lens through which the vulnerabilities of democracies under strain can be understood.

The paradox of the Depression is that while it struck almost every nation with comparable economic force, it fractured political systems unevenly. Some democracies endured, battered but intact, while others collapsed into authoritarianism. The crisis exposed democracy's central weakness: its dependence on trust, patience, and institutions that are neither inevitable nor indestructible. In moments of mass desperation, the slow grind of parliamentary debate could appear pitiful next to the drama of leaders who promised certainty, unity, and action.

This chapter begins with patterns that spanned nations. From Weimar Germany to the French Third Republic, from Britain's coalition politics to America's contested reforms, democracies struggled to translate economic emergency into coherent policy. The Depression was not simply a fiscal challenge; it was a psychological and cultural earthquake. When work disappeared and savings evaporated, so too did the sense of belonging and control that democracy requires to function. Voters began to seek not deliberation but deliverance.

Why, then, did extremes flourish? Authoritarian movements thrived not only on hunger and unemployment but on identity—on the promise of restored greatness, reclaimed order, or protection from imagined enemies. Where democratic leaders hesitated, authoritarians staged certainty. Where legislatures splintered, strongmen declared unity. It was not reasoned argument that prevailed but the seduction of clarity in a world that seemed otherwise unknowable. The Depression revealed how economic collapse could be transmuted into moral panic, how despair could be channelled into allegiance to extremes.

At the heart of this comparison lies the contrast between America and Germany. Both suffered deeply, yet their institutional responses diverged. In the United States, the Constitution and its political traditions, though strained, held enough resilience to absorb Roosevelt's sweeping experiments. In Germany, by contrast, the brittle Weimar system fractured under pressure, its institutions incapable of channelling discontent into constructive reform. The lesson is structural: democracies are not tested in their prosperity but in their collapse, and survival depends less on ideals than on institutional design and adaptability.

Institutions under pressure reveal their true strength—or weakness. Robust frameworks, rooted in legitimacy and public trust, can absorb shock and adapt. Fragile ones, built on shallow consent or partisan rancour, crumble quickly. The Depression showed that elections alone do not guarantee survival; it is the scaffolding of law, accountability, and civic trust that allows democracies to bend without breaking. Yet the temptation of authoritarianism always lurks, promising speed where democracy stumbles, decisiveness where democracy hesitates.

The story of the 1930s, then, is not merely about the fall of specific regimes but about a recurring human dilemma: how societies respond when democracy feels inadequate to crisis. This chapter probes that dilemma through comparative lessons, institutional analysis, and the enduring question of why, when fear eclipses hope, democracies so easily give way to extremes. The answers are not confined to history. They speak to the fragility of trust, the allure of certainty, and the precarious balance on which democratic survival has always rested.

The reader will find here not just accounts of collapse but insights into endurance. For democracies, the Depression was both a trial and a revelation: it showed the cost of weakness, the possibilities of resilience, and the enduring shadow of authoritarian temptation. Whether nations turn inward toward democracy's principles or outward toward its alternatives remains the unresolved question that echoes far beyond the 1930s—into our own unsettled times.

Patterns Across Nations

In the winter of 1931, queues outside relief offices in Chicago and Berlin bore a haunting similarity: men in heavy coats, faces lined with hunger and humiliation, waiting not for wages but for sustenance. Yet within a decade, the countries they stood in would diverge profoundly—one reviving its democratic institutions, the other surrendering to dictatorship. The paradox is stark: the same global depression, the same collapse of trade and employment, but radically different political outcomes. Why did democracies stumble everywhere, yet fall only in some places?

The Great Depression was not a single national tragedy but a shared global rupture, experienced in diverse political climates. From the industrial belts of Britain to the agrarian plains of Poland, elected governments found themselves incapable of reconciling mass expectations with shrinking revenues. Liberal economies, once hailed for their openness, suddenly appeared brittle. Parliamentary institutions, reliant on negotiation and compromise, seemed ill-suited to moments of emergency. Yet these crises unfolded differently: some democracies clung to life, others imploded, and still others became hybrid systems, part-democratic, part-authoritarian, straining under the weight of public anger.

The comparative lesson begins with commonality: all democracies faced the dual crisis of economics and legitimacy. The Depression destroyed not only jobs but the credibility of those who governed. In Britain, the unemployment lines of Jarrow or Merthyr Tydfil fuelled despair but did not dismantle parliamentary continuity. In Germany, by contrast, chronic instability within the Weimar Republic provided fertile ground for extremists to promise deliverance. France stumbled, its Third Republic fractious and weakened, yet it endured until external defeat in 1940 rather than internal collapse. The same pressures produced contrasting outcomes, revealing the variable strength of democratic foundations.

One decisive factor lay in institutional resilience. Systems that commanded deep-rooted legitimacy could withstand frustration, however severe. Britain's monarchy, Parliament, and civil service provided a framework that, though unimaginative, commanded public trust. America's Constitution allowed Roosevelt to expand executive power in extraordinary ways while still cloaking reform in the language of continuity. By contrast, Weimar Germany lacked both tradition and consensus. Its constitution contained loopholes that enabled presidential emergency decrees, and its fragmented party system turned legislatures into arenas of paralysis. Economic depression alone did not destroy democracy; rather, it exposed where democracy was already fragile.

Another key variable was the narrative of blame. Democracies that managed to channel public anger towards external or structural causes fared better than those where elites turned on each other. In the United States, Roosevelt's fireside chats reframed despair as a shared struggle that required collective action. In Germany, nationalist demagogues redirected rage towards scapegoats—Jews, communists, Versailles—turning economic grievance into political mobilisation for extremism. The Depression thus acted not simply as a material crisis but as a battlefield of narratives, with survival depending on who defined the meaning of collapse.

Yet even where democracy endured, it often did so at the cost of its dynamism. Britain's National Government, formed in 1931, preserved parliamentary structures but drained politics of real contest, narrowing the scope of debate to the management of decline. In France, chronic coalition-building left governments too fragile to act decisively, perpetuating the impression of drift. Survival did not necessarily mean vitality; many democracies lived on in muted, defensive form, their citizens more resigned than inspired.

These comparative patterns illuminate a larger truth: democracy is not a static inheritance but a living system, tested most acutely in moments of scarcity. It depends on patience, but patience is a fragile commodity when hunger gnaws and savings vanish. When societies demand swift remedies, the slow, procedural logic of democratic governance appears inadequate. It is in such moments that alternatives—often authoritarian, always simplistic—gain their appeal.

The Depression demonstrated both democracy's vulnerability and its endurance. It showed how identical economic shocks could produce radically different political trajectories, depending on institutions, narratives, and traditions. More importantly, it revealed that democratic survival is never guaranteed; it rests on the delicate balance between legitimacy and performance, trust and capacity.

The unresolved question lingers: if another systemic crisis were to shatter economies and unsettle societies, which democracies would endure and which would fracture? The 1930s suggest no universal answer, only a warning—that fragility is the norm, resilience the exception, and the patterns of collapse are always waiting to reassert themselves.

Why Extremes Flourished

On the evening of 30 January 1933, as Adolf Hitler was sworn in as Chancellor of Germany, crowds surged through Berlin with torches held high, cheering the dawn of what they believed would be national renewal. To outsiders, the spectacle was unsettling: why should a nation of poets and engineers turn to a man whose politics were steeped in violence and scapegoating? Yet to many Germans, battered by years of economic collapse and humiliation, extremism did not feel irrational—it felt like deliverance. The Depression had not merely destroyed livelihoods; it had stripped away identity, dignity, and trust in the centre.

The paradox of the 1930s is that extremism flourished not only in places of deep misery but also where collective fear eclipsed individual suffering. In Germany, unemployment peaked at nearly six million, but it was the sense of national degradation—rooted in the Versailles settlement and intensified by economic collapse—that gave Hitler's rhetoric such force. Across the Atlantic, Americans faced breadlines and farm foreclosures, yet democracy endured, in part because Roosevelt's New Deal gave people a narrative of inclusion rather than exclusion. Extremism, then, was never only about hunger; it was about the psychological need for certainty, belonging, and a story of redemption.

Economic catastrophe acted as a solvent, dissolving the credibility of moderate politics. When centrist parties called for austerity or compromise, they appeared feeble in the face of chaos. Extremists, by contrast, offered clarity: a defined enemy, a plan of action, a promise of swift reversal. The Nazis insisted Germany's woes stemmed from Jews, Marxists, and foreign conspiracies. Italian Fascists spoke of decadence overcome by discipline. In Japan, militarists preached that scarcity could be solved through conquest. Each of these movements distilled complexity into certainty, and in uncertain times, that clarity carried intoxicating appeal.

Identity deepened this dynamic. Economic collapse does not strike all groups equally; it magnifies existing divisions. In multi-ethnic states like Germany, scapegoating minorities became a mechanism for reasserting a wounded national self. In Eastern Europe, where fragile democracies struggled to hold together diverse populations, politics polarised along ethnic and class lines, paving the way for authoritarian regimes that promised cohesion at the expense of pluralism. By contrast, in more homogeneous societies with stronger traditions of inclusive identity—such as the United States or Scandinavia—democracy proved harder to uproot, though not immune to strains.

Extremes flourished because they offered more than policies—they offered belonging. Political rallies, uniforms, and symbols created a sense of collective power that compensated for individual despair. A worker without wages could still feel valued as part of a marching column; a farmer facing foreclosure could find solace in a movement that promised to restore his dignity. Extremist politics became a kind of theatre of hope, where even the disenfranchised could imagine themselves actors in a national drama of renewal.

Yet this was not inevitable. Where credible leadership filled the vacuum with pragmatic reform, extremism was blunted. Roosevelt's fireside chats transformed the language of crisis from fear to solidarity, reasserting trust in democratic institutions. In Britain, the monarchy and Parliament provided continuity, dulling the allure of radical movements. The lesson is stark: economics may create the conditions for extremism, but political psychology—how leaders narrate crisis, how societies frame identity—determines whether the extremes take root.

The flourishing of extremes during the Depression thus reveals a deeper truth about democracy: it is not destroyed by poverty alone, but by the erosion of hope. When citizens lose faith that moderation can deliver, they seek certainty elsewhere, even at the cost of liberty. That is why the Depression remains more than a historical episode; it is a warning about the fragility of balance in democratic life.

The unresolved question remains: in a future crisis, would the centre hold, or would the extremes once again seduce societies with promises of clarity, belonging, and strength? The 1930s suggest that the danger lies not only in material deprivation, but in the hunger for meaning that grows when democracies falter.

Case Study Contrasts: America and Germany

In the early 1930s, two nations stood at the edge of collapse. Both were democracies on paper. Both endured catastrophic economic dislocation, staggering unemployment, and a crisis of confidence in their political institutions. Yet their trajectories could not have been more divergent. In Washington, Franklin Roosevelt's inauguration in March 1933 was marked not by torches and martial anthems, but by a calm assertion of faith: "the only thing we have to fear is fear itself." In Berlin, less than two months earlier, Adolf Hitler had been appointed Chancellor, greeted by a sea of flags and flames as his supporters celebrated the beginning of dictatorship. The Depression had tested democracy in both nations, but while the United States bent, Germany broke.

Why did one democracy endure while the other collapsed? The contrast is not merely of historical curiosity; it exposes the structures, habits, and narratives that sustain or undermine free societies under pressure. America and Germany offer, side by side, a lesson in how crisis magnifies both the strengths and the weaknesses embedded in a nation's political culture.

In Germany, the Depression struck an already fragile state. The Weimar Republic, born in the ashes of the First World War and burdened by Versailles reparations, never enjoyed full legitimacy in the eyes of its citizens. For many, democracy was less an achievement than a humiliation imposed from outside. Parliamentary politics were fragmented, with dozens of parties competing, coalition governments collapsing in rapid succession, and extremists exploiting every stalemate. When the Depression drove unemployment above six million and businesses into bankruptcy, the public saw not resilience but dysfunction. The centre could not hold; by 1930, extremist parties commanded a third of the Reichstag.

The United States faced an economic crisis of similar magnitude—by 1933, one in four Americans was unemployed, banks were failing by the thousands, and shantytowns spread across the landscape. Yet the constitutional system, battered though it was, retained popular loyalty. Unlike Weimar Germany, the American Republic carried the weight of more than a century of continuity. The presidency, Congress, and the courts were seen not as foreign impositions but as native institutions. This legitimacy gave Roosevelt space to experiment, even to stretch constitutional norms, without dissolving democratic consent.

Personality mattered too, but it was inseparable from structure. Hitler's rise was facilitated by elites who thought they could contain him, by a constitution that allowed presidential decrees to bypass parliament, and by a culture accustomed to hierarchy. Roosevelt, by contrast, channelled crisis into a language of inclusion. His fireside chats were not mere rhetoric; they wove the public into the fabric of government action. Programmes like the Civilian Conservation Corps and Social Security provided not just jobs and relief, but a sense of shared endeavour. Where German democracy fractured into competing identities, American democracy reasserted a unifying story.

Economic orthodoxy also divided the two cases. German governments clung to austerity, convinced that balanced budgets were the only path to stability. The result was further contraction, deepening misery, and fuelling radicalism. In the United States, orthodoxy gave way to pragmatism. Roosevelt abandoned the gold standard, tolerated deficits, and experimented with bold interventions. The New Deal was less coherent policy than a philosophy of action: better to try and fail than to stand paralysed. This willingness to adapt gave democracy a chance to prove its relevance.

But the divergence cannot be explained by policy alone. At root lay the psychology of the people and the narratives available to them. Germans, reeling from defeat in war and the punitive terms of Versailles, were primed to believe that democracy equalled weakness, that only strong leadership could restore pride. Americans, despite hardship, still carried a cultural memory of resilience—of pioneers, of self-reliance, of the Constitution as the vessel of liberty. The Depression could shake confidence, but it did not uproot identity.

The contrast also underscores how elites respond under pressure. German conservatives, terrified of communism and desperate to preserve their privileges, struck their Faustian bargain with Hitler, imagining they could harness his movement. American elites, though divided, largely accepted Roosevelt's reforms as the price of preserving the system. Compromise in one case stabilised democracy; in the other, it destroyed it.

What these two paths reveal is that democracy is never tested only by economics. It is tested by the interplay of structure, culture, and imagination. Crisis can expose fragility, as in Germany, where the Weimar system's weaknesses collapsed under strain. But it can also catalyse reinvention, as in the United States, where democratic institutions proved elastic enough to accommodate new solutions.

The question that lingers is unsettling: in moments of future upheaval, which model will democracies follow? Will they fracture under the weight of fear, or will they adapt, finding in crisis the impetus to renew themselves? The Depression leaves no comforting answer, only the stark lesson that survival is never guaranteed—and collapse, once begun, can be swift.

Institutions Under Pressure

The Great Depression did not simply test economies; it tested the scaffolding of political and social order. The collapse of markets revealed something deeper: that institutions—the courts, parliaments, central banks, unions, even churches—were not neutral containers but living systems whose resilience or fragility determined whether societies bent or broke. Some institutions absorbed shock, adapted, and emerged scarred but intact. Others splintered under pressure, exposing fissures long hidden beneath the surface. The Depression was thus not just an economic crisis but an X-ray, revealing the hidden strengths and fatal weaknesses of democratic systems.

Consider the fate of Germany's Weimar Republic. Its constitution had been hailed as one of the most modern in Europe, yet by 1930 it had become a vehicle for authoritarian decrees. Article 48, originally designed as a safeguard for emergencies, allowed the president to bypass parliament—a provision tolerable in stability but lethal under crisis. Economic collapse turned legal ambiguity into political rupture. Institutions that lacked legitimacy in the public's imagination were the first to wither. Courts were mistrusted, parties fragmented, and civil service officials leaned toward authoritarianism. When millions faced hunger and unemployment, citizens judged not the theories behind institutions but their tangible ability to deliver. Weimar's failure was less a sudden implosion than the slow erosion of trust.

Contrast this with the United States, where institutions faced comparable pressures yet adapted. Banks collapsed by the thousands, but the Federal Reserve and Treasury improvised new roles. Congress, paralysed in the Hoover years, found renewed energy once Roosevelt took office. The Supreme Court resisted elements of the New Deal, striking down key legislation, but here too resilience revealed itself: Roosevelt's attempt to "pack" the Court in 1937 failed, yet the justices shifted course in what became known as the "switch in time that saved nine." Institutional rigidity yielded to pragmatism. Where Weimar's clauses facilitated collapse, America's checks and balances bent without breaking.

The British case illustrates another pattern: institutions that survive by retreating into tradition. The Depression struck hardest at the North, but the parliamentary system, insulated by habit and by the monarchy's symbolic weight, endured. When the Labour government splintered in 1931, the creation of a National Government was less innovation than a reassertion of establishment continuity. Parliament did not solve the crisis; it managed it. What kept the system intact was not dynamism but legitimacy rooted in centuries of precedent. The lesson is paradoxical: institutional survival does not always require radical reform, so long as the public believes in the theatre of continuity.

What makes institutions resilient? Partly, their capacity to adapt rules without appearing to betray them. The gold standard, once sacrosanct, was abandoned by Britain in 1931. This move could have been framed as constitutional heresy, undermining confidence in sterling and the Bank of England. Instead, it was managed as a pragmatic adjustment, enabling institutions to absorb the shock while maintaining their authority. Flexibility cloaked in continuity allowed British financial structures to reconfigure without rupture.

Yet resilience is not simply institutional design; it is also cultural habit. In Scandinavia, the Depression drove states toward social democracy rather than extremism. Why? Their parliaments had traditions of compromise, their societies strong local networks of trust. Institutions there were not abstract rules but extensions of social practice. By contrast, in countries with sharp class divides and little history of consensus—Spain, for example—crisis ignited polarisation that institutions could not contain.

The Depression also highlights a cruel truth: institutions often prove weakest where they are most needed. Central banks failed to stabilise credit precisely when economies required liquidity. Parliaments deadlocked when bold legislation was urgent. Trade unions fractured under unemployment pressures. The irony is stark: the very institutions designed to moderate crisis became accelerants of instability when their legitimacy or flexibility failed.

At a deeper level lies the philosophical question of institutional trust. Institutions rest on collective belief in their authority. They do not endure merely by wielding force; they endure because people accept their decisions as binding. The Depression corroded this faith. Where citizens perceived institutions as instruments of the elite or incapable of protection, they turned to alternatives: radical parties, charismatic leaders, or even violence in the streets. Where institutions maintained a connection to the everyday struggles of citizens, they could preserve loyalty even when delivering imperfect results.

The global pattern, then, is neither uniform collapse nor uniform survival. Rather, the Depression revealed that resilience depends on a combination of design, adaptability, and legitimacy. Fragile states with fragmented party systems and brittle constitutions fell first. Systems with entrenched traditions or mechanisms of adaptation muddled through. Yet even in the "success stories," scars remained. The United States emerged with a larger federal state than ever before. Britain leaned more heavily on empire.

Scandinavia deepened its welfare structures. In each case, institutions survived by becoming something slightly different from what they had been before.

The lesson remains as unsettling as it is instructive: no institution is tested in the abstract. It is tested when unemployment surges, when banks fail, when fear becomes a daily presence. Under such pressure, paper rules and historical prestige matter less than whether citizens can still believe that the system belongs to them. And so we are left with a lingering question: when the next global crisis arrives, will today's institutions prove supple enough to adapt—or brittle enough to break?

The Authoritarian Temptation

In the autumn of 1930, queues for bread in Berlin stretched around corners once lined with bustling shops. Trams clattered by half-empty, carrying men who clutched not briefcases but crumpled notices of dismissal. Democracy, once held up as the harbinger of prosperity and stability after the Great War, looked increasingly like a hollow promise. Into this void strode men with uniforms, flags, and simple slogans. While parliaments debated austerity packages and currency controls, authoritarian leaders offered certainty: jobs, order, and national pride. The appeal was not merely political but psychological, reaching deep into the human craving for security when the world seems to fracture.

The paradox is stark. At the very moment when societies most needed deliberation, patience, and collective negotiation—the lifeblood of democracy—people were least willing to tolerate the slowness of such processes. Authoritarianism, with its crisp commands and symbolic rituals, appeared efficient by comparison. When a single leader could promise clarity in a single sentence, parliamentary debate seemed like a cruel indulgence. In this way, the Depression exposed a weakness at the heart of democratic governance: its reliance on uncertainty as both a virtue and a vulnerability.

Authoritarian promises took many forms, but they shared a common grammar. Mussolini declared that he had made the trains run on time. Hitler vowed to abolish unemployment through rearmament and public works. Stalin insisted that planning, not markets, would eliminate scarcity. Each promise was absolute, framed as a cure rather than a compromise. The attraction lay not in the plausibility of the policies—few citizens understood the mechanics of economic revival—but in the aura of certainty. People were less seduced by technical details than by the sheer relief of believing someone knew the way forward.

Economic desperation amplified this allure. In Germany, unemployment peaked at nearly six million by early 1932, leaving entire families dependent on soup kitchens. Democracy was experienced not as a principle but as a lived reality of insecurity. By contrast, Nazi rallies offered not only political theatre but communal belonging: a chance to transform personal humiliation into collective pride. In Italy, Fascism channelled anxieties about modernity and decline into a vision of rebirth, where sacrifice for the nation gave meaning to individual suffering. Even in societies less radicalised, from Spain to Hungary, the rhetoric of strongmen framed hesitation and debate as luxuries a crisis-stricken world could not afford.

Yet the temptation of authoritarian certainty was not solely economic. It was existential. Democracies ask their citizens to accept ambiguity: that outcomes are contested, that policies may fail, that tomorrow is not guaranteed. Under prosperity, this openness feels liberating. Under collapse, it feels intolerable. In such conditions, people yearn for a world without doubt, where suffering can be explained by enemies—foreigners, traitors, bankers, communists—rather than by the complexity of structural breakdowns. Authoritarian leaders supplied not just programmes but narratives, scapegoats, and a story in which chaos had a villain and the nation a saviour.

There were, of course, those who resisted. In the United States, Roosevelt's New Deal demonstrated that democratic systems could also project certainty, albeit in a different register. Fireside chats, alphabet agencies, and bold experiments created the impression of direction and purpose, even as policies shifted in trial-and-error fashion. What distinguished Roosevelt's response from authoritarian models was not the absence of uncertainty but the willingness to manage it openly. He framed struggle as a collective journey rather than a surrender to a commanding will. It was a precarious balance: too much hesitation would have fed despair, but too much rigidity would have bred resentment. Roosevelt succeeded in making democracy feel active rather than paralysed.

The Depression also reveals how institutions mediate the authoritarian temptation. Where courts, parliaments, and local governments were already mistrusted, citizens abandoned them quickly. Where institutions enjoyed residual legitimacy, people were more willing to endure hardship. The key was not perfection but credibility. Britain's parliamentary system was derided for its elitism, yet it retained a symbolic authority that cushioned the crisis. In Germany, by contrast, Weimar institutions carried little historical weight and were tainted by association with wartime defeat. Certainty from an authoritarian leader thus seemed more trustworthy than the faltering compromises of an unloved system.

Philosophically, the authoritarian temptation speaks to an enduring human dilemma: the tension between freedom and security. Freedom entails risk—the risk of disagreement, delay, and imperfection. Security promises resolution, but at the cost of autonomy. The Depression pushed this dilemma to breaking point. Millions who had once tolerated the risks of freedom concluded that the costs had become unbearable. Better, they thought, to surrender liberty to a decisive hand than to drown in the sea of democratic drift.

But the very strength of authoritarian promises was also their fragility. Certainty, once pledged, must be delivered. Hitler's regime survived its early years because rearmament and public works reduced unemployment; Mussolini's endured because propaganda masked stagnation with spectacle. Yet such systems thrived only so long as they could maintain the illusion of control. The gamble of authoritarianism is that certainty is rarely sustainable in a complex world. It can mobilise societies in the short term, but it risks catastrophe when confronted with realities that no decree can erase.

The Depression thus offers more than a historical lesson; it warns of a recurring temptation. In times of upheaval, people do not simply seek solutions. They seek sureness. When democracies falter in providing reassurance, authoritarians step forward with the easy clarity of absolutes. The question, then, is not whether people will be drawn to such promises—they will—but whether societies can strengthen their democratic institutions to project resilience without succumbing to illusion.

That unresolved tension remains. Can democracies ever persuade citizens that uncertainty is not weakness but strength, that freedom's risks are worth enduring even in the bleakest times? Or will the next great crisis once again make the certainties of authoritarianism feel irresistible? The Depression left this question hanging over the twentieth century—and it continues to haunt the twenty-first.

Chapter 9

Global Lessons in Collapse

In the summer of 1931, the queues outside Austrian banks lengthened by the hour. What had begun as a rumour—that the venerable Creditanstalt was failing—soon turned into panic. Customers pressed against locked doors, desperate to withdraw savings that no longer existed. Within weeks, the crisis leapt borders: the German banking system faltered, sterling trembled, and the gold standard itself teetered. The chain reaction was not confined to the ledgers. Governments toppled, parliaments gridlocked, and in streets from Vienna to Berlin, extremists gained audiences they had once only dreamed of. It was an object lesson in how quickly financial fragility could translate into political collapse.

The paradox was brutal: money, the abstract fabric of trust on which modern economies were built, proved both indispensable and astonishingly fragile. When that fabric tore, the damage was not limited to investors or bankers—it corroded the confidence that held entire polities together. For millions, the Depression was not an academic curve of declining GDP but a visceral experience of fear: wages vanishing, savings evaporating, futures narrowing. Out of that fear, politics shifted. Where democratic leaders dithered, radicals promised clarity. Where international cooperation failed, nationalism hardened. The crisis was not merely about economics—it was about imagination, about what people could believe was possible or tolerable in their societies.

Economic collapse, in this sense, was both weapon and catalyst. Governments used emergency to justify repression, while movements exploited misery to advance ideologies once considered fringe. In Italy and Germany, authoritarian leaders cast themselves as saviours capable of transforming despair into destiny. In Britain and America, elites scrambled for stability, turning to coalitions or experimental reforms. The contrasts matter less as separate histories than as variations on a common theme: the

Depression revealed that when prosperity vanishes, political systems are forced to show what they are made of.

If fear drove authoritarian temptations, hope provided the counterweight. Roosevelt's fireside chats in the United States were less about policy detail than about narrative: he convinced millions that government had a plan, even if the details were improvisational. In Scandinavia, social democratic parties bound reform to solidarity, showing that democracy could adapt rather than collapse. These cultural narratives mattered as much as unemployment figures. Austerity framed as unavoidable doom corroded trust; hardship framed as a shared challenge could inspire resilience. What societies chose to believe about themselves often determined whether they slid into extremism or found paths to renewal.

But while individual states improvised, the international stage told a darker story. The League of Nations, designed to foster cooperation, proved impotent when it was most needed. Member states clung to national interests, retreating into protectionism and currency blocs rather than pooling solutions. The collapse of free trade into tariffs and quotas deepened the spiral. Economic nationalism fed geopolitical aggression: Japan seized Manchuria to secure markets; Germany cast its expansion as Lebensraum; Britain and France leaned harder on their empires. The global crisis, unmanaged, became both justification and fuel for war.

To study the 1930s, then, is not merely to revisit a bygone disaster but to confront a perennial truth: crises rarely stay contained. They spill across borders, destabilise institutions, and reconfigure political imaginations. The Depression was not simply an economic calamity but a rehearsal for conflict, demonstrating how scarcity and fear could be marshalled into aggression. Its lessons resonate uneasily today, in a world where financial shocks, pandemics, and climate disruptions again test both national institutions and international cooperation.

This chapter traces those lessons, from the collapse of orthodoxies to the rise of extremes, from the failures of global governance to the pathways that led directly to war. It asks not only how democracies stumbled and authoritarians rose, but why fear and hope carried such different weight depending on the stories nations told themselves. And it closes by turning toward our own age, where the echoes of the 1930s remind us that economic fragility is never merely about numbers: it is about power, belief, and the choices societies make under pressure.

The Depression has too often been treated as a contained tragedy, a prelude neatly bounded by recovery or war. In truth, it was a mirror—showing how civilisation behaves when the floor beneath it gives way. The task now is not to admire or condemn the past from a safe distance, but to ask whether we have built stronger foundations, or whether we remain just as vulnerable to the authoritarian temptation, the collapse of cooperation, and the politics of fear. The answer is not given; it must be tested, as it always has been, in the storms yet to come.

Economic Fragility as a Political Weapon

In 1931, when Austria's largest bank, Creditanstalt, collapsed under the weight of bad debts, the tremors rippled far beyond Vienna. Markets seized, currencies wobbled, and trust dissolved almost overnight. Yet what mattered most was not the bankruptcy itself but the political avalanche it unleashed: governments resigned, parties fractured, and extremists exploited the moment to argue that democracy was incapable of protecting its citizens. A financial failure had become a weapon in political struggle—a reminder that economic fragility is never neutral, never confined to balance sheets. It reshapes the very terms of legitimacy.

This was hardly the first time material insecurity had been converted into political force. Throughout history, leaders have recognised that the fear of hunger or ruin can be far more potent than the abstractions of ideology. What distinguished the Great Depression was its global reach and the speed with which economic trauma destabilised entire polities. In Germany, collapsing trade and mass unemployment fuelled the Nazi claim that only a disciplined, authoritarian order could restore national strength. In Britain, the sterling crisis fractured parties and forced a coalition, but it also narrowed the political imagination to management rather than reform. In the United States, despair opened the door to Roosevelt's New Deal—proof that fragility could also be harnessed toward renewal.

The Depression revealed a paradox: economic crisis could either fracture democratic systems or provide the impetus to strengthen them. Much depended on whether institutions and leaders could channel insecurity into constructive action or whether they allowed panic to metastasise into cynicism. When parliaments appeared paralysed, populists and strongmen could weaponise economic collapse to delegitimise the very idea of compromise. The failures of the Weimar Republic exemplify this dynamic: each round of austerity deepened unemployment, which in turn amplified extremist propaganda. Fragility became not only the condition of politics but its language.

Economic weakness is not a passive backdrop—it actively shapes political narratives. In Japan, the export collapse of 1930–31 was not merely a crisis of trade; it became ammunition for militarists who insisted that parliamentary dithering endangered national survival. In their rhetoric, hunger at home justified conquest abroad. The fragility of markets was reframed as evidence of the fragility of civilian government. By contrast, in Scandinavia, social democrats succeeded in redefining crisis as an argument for solidarity. Through welfare expansion and negotiated compromises, they neutralised the weapon of fear by offering a plausible alternative vision.

The weaponisation of fragility also thrived on identity. Economic downturns rarely distribute pain evenly. In the 1930s, minorities, immigrants, and ideological opponents were cast as scapegoats. In Germany, Jews were vilified as both capitalists and communists—an impossible contradiction that nevertheless thrived because insecurity made absurdities palatable if they promised certainty. In the United States, racialised narratives of deserving and undeserving poor influenced both relief distribution and political discourse. Fragility, when politicised, sharpened boundaries between "insiders" and "outsiders," between the imagined community of the nation and those blamed for its decline.

Underlying this was the philosophical tension between contingency and control. Democracies, by design, are systems of negotiation, improvisation, and pluralism. But in times of economic collapse, citizens often crave certainty: a clear plan, a single voice, a sense that someone is in control. Authoritarian leaders exploit this craving by converting fragility into a case for centralisation. Their argument is seductively simple: chaos is the fault of weak institutions; stability requires obedience. Fragility thus becomes not just a danger but an opportunity—a stage on which authoritarians can enact the drama of rescue.

Yet fragility can also expose the hollowness of authoritarian claims. The Soviet Union trumpeted its insulation from capitalist collapse, presenting central planning as proof of resilience. To many observers abroad, this seemed persuasive. But inside the USSR, fragility was managed not through prosperity but through repression, famine, and coercion. Economic weakness was not solved but concealed, redirected into propaganda. Here lies the deeper lesson: fragility can be a political weapon for democracies and dictatorships alike, but the price paid by societies differs dramatically depending on how that weapon is wielded.

The Great Depression demonstrates that fragility is not merely an episode of vulnerability but a recurring condition of modern economies. Markets are inherently volatile; global trade links mean shocks travel fast. What varies is the political use made of that volatility. Do leaders frame crisis as evidence of democratic inadequacy or as justification for expanding democratic capacity? Do citizens interpret fragility as a call for solidarity or as licence for suspicion? The answers shape not just elections but the survival of systems.

The unresolved question is whether modern societies have learned to defuse fragility as a weapon. Contemporary crises—from financial crashes to pandemics—still show how swiftly economic insecurity can be converted into political capital for extremes. The Depression warns us that fragility will always be a battlefield, not a passing inconvenience. The challenge is not whether fragility can be avoided—it cannot—but whether its political exploitation can be contained before it corrodes the very foundations of governance. The weapon is always at hand. The real question is: who will wield it, and to what end?

Fear and Hope in Public Consciousness

In 1933, as Franklin Roosevelt delivered his inaugural address in Washington, declaring that "the only thing we have to fear is fear itself," another leader was making his presence felt in Berlin. Adolf Hitler, newly appointed Chancellor, offered Germans a radically different message: that fear was justified, that enemies within and without stalked the nation, and that only through strength, exclusion, and obedience could survival be secured. Both men spoke to societies battered by the same global crisis. Both mobilised emotion, myth, and imagination. Yet one invoked hope as a tool of reform, while the other entrenched fear as the foundation of extremism. The divergence is a reminder that economic hardship alone does not determine a society's path—cultural narratives, and the way they are internalised, tip the balance.

Fear and hope are not opposites so much as twin energies that shape collective consciousness. Crises amplify them both. When millions lost jobs, homes, and savings during the Great Depression, fear was inevitable—fear of hunger, of downward mobility, of a future stripped of dignity. But whether that fear turned into paralysis, scapegoating, or collective renewal depended on the stories leaders and movements told. In Germany, the Nazi narrative fused fear with national humiliation, making despair feel like evidence of betrayal. In the United States, the New Deal sought to reframe insecurity as a challenge that government, working with citizens, could meet. Fear pushed both societies to the edge; hope determined which way they leaned.

The potency of cultural narrative lay in its ability to humanise abstract economic forces. Falling commodity prices or collapsing trade were technical realities. But what mattered politically was how people understood their suffering. Did they view hardship as an assault from faceless markets, as the failure of corrupt elites, or as the misfortune of a global storm requiring solidarity? In Britain, despite hardship, narratives of resilience and imperial responsibility helped contain radicalism, at least temporarily. In Latin America, by contrast, the Depression encouraged nationalist movements that portrayed foreign capital as exploitative, feeding populist currents that reshaped politics for decades.

Fear, when weaponised, draws its power from simplicity. It thrives on scapegoats, clear enemies, and promises of quick remedies. The unemployed man does not need to untangle the gold standard's technicalities; he is told his hunger is the fault of the banker, the foreigner, or the political traitor. Hope, by contrast, demands a more complex narrative: that patient reform, shared sacrifice, and institutional adaptation can deliver results. It is harder to sell, because it requires trust in systems that may already have failed. In times of acute insecurity, fear's bluntness often outpaces hope's nuance. Yet the survival of democracy rests precisely on the ability to keep hope credible.

The psychological dimension cannot be overlooked. Fear narrows vision; it primes individuals to protect what little they have left. Hope broadens perspective; it encourages investment in futures that seem uncertain. When societies fall into cycles of fear, they become less tolerant of ambiguity, more hostile to compromise, and more receptive to authoritarian solutions. In Weimar Germany, this manifested in the erosion of parliamentary trust and the search for a saviour. In Roosevelt's America, hope was ritualised through fireside chats, public works programmes, and cultural initiatives that reminded people they were not abandoned. The difference lay not in material conditions alone but in the ability of leadership to direct imagination.

There is also a philosophical truth at stake: fear and hope are not mere reactions but choices, often cultivated through institutions. Schools, churches, unions, newspapers, and political parties all played roles in shaping how ordinary people made sense of their hardship. Where unions fostered solidarity, despair could be translated into collective bargaining and reformist politics. Where media amplified conspiracy, fear metastasised into paranoia and extremism. Narratives did not simply mirror the economic reality; they constructed it, endowing collapse with meaning that could either divide or unite.

The Depression revealed how fragile the boundary is between the constructive and destructive uses of fear. Roosevelt himself drew on fear—but redirected it toward the fear of fear, turning anxiety into a rallying cry for courage. In contrast, fascist movements insisted that fear was proof of danger and required purges, militarisation, and obedience. Both strategies recognised that fear could not be ignored; what differed was the political architecture built around it. Hope is not the absence of fear, but its transformation into something bearable, even generative.

Today, the lesson lingers. Modern crises—financial meltdowns, pandemics, climate shocks—generate both fear and hope. What determines outcomes is not the scale of the disruption but the quality of the stories societies tell themselves. If fear becomes a drumbeat of division, authoritarianism finds fertile ground. If hope is cultivated through institutions that deliver visible support and collective meaning, even the harshest storms can strengthen democracy. The Great Depression shows us that public consciousness is not a passive mirror of material life; it is an arena of contest, where fear and hope wrestle for dominance.

The lingering question remains: in times of profound uncertainty, which voice will carry louder—the one that demands exclusion and obedience, or the one that invites trust and renewal? The answer is rarely predetermined. It lies in the narratives societies are willing to believe, and the leaders bold enough to craft them. Fear will always be present. The survival of democracy depends on whether hope can be made persuasive enough to compete.

The Limits of International Cooperation

In September 1931, Japanese troops staged the Mukden Incident and swiftly seized Manchuria, brushing aside the fragile mechanisms of international order. Within weeks, the League of Nations was confronted with its most serious test. Here was naked aggression by a member state against another's sovereign territory, a violation of the very principles on which the League had been built. Yet as months dragged on and fact-finding commissions deliberated, Japan consolidated its hold, established the puppet state of Manchukuo, and eventually walked away from the League altogether. The lesson was stark: the institution that had been conceived to prevent precisely this scenario had neither the resolve nor the unity to act decisively.

The paralysis of the League was not merely the result of apathy. It reflected structural weaknesses embedded in the very design of interwar international cooperation. The League had been born out of idealism, championed by Woodrow Wilson, but its architecture depended on the participation of the very powers least willing to subordinate national interest to collective will. The United States never joined; Britain and France, both struggling with economic depression and political fragility, were hesitant to act in ways that might impose costs on their own overstretched empires. Smaller states, meanwhile, lacked the military or economic clout to compel obedience. The lofty rhetoric of Geneva masked an uncomfortable truth: international cooperation without enforcement power was little more than moral theatre.

The economic crisis deepened these fissures. When the Depression struck, nations retreated behind protective tariffs, competitive devaluations, and bilateral trade agreements. International collaboration, already tenuous, became a liability. Why should governments facing mass unemployment sacrifice domestic relief to uphold distant norms? The Ottawa Conference of 1932, which inaugurated imperial preference for Britain and its dominions, symbolised this inward turn. While the League talked of collective economic measures, the major powers pursued national recovery through insular strategies. Economic self-preservation trumped any notion of global responsibility.

This weakness was not only practical but psychological. The Depression generated a climate of insecurity in which fear eclipsed the spirit of internationalism that had briefly flourished after 1919. The very idea of shared governance seemed alien in a world where survival appeared to depend on border controls and protectionist walls. Citizens demanded immediate relief, not abstract commitments to global order. Leaders responded accordingly, prioritising national constituencies over fragile international promises. As the Depression wore on, the League was less a guardian of peace than a mirror of political fragmentation.

The League's handling of aggression in Ethiopia in 1935 further illustrated its impotence. When Mussolini's Italy launched an unprovoked invasion, the League responded with sanctions—but carefully crafted ones that excluded vital commodities such as oil, designed not to provoke Italian withdrawal from the alliance against Germany. The sanctions failed; Ethiopia fell, and the credibility of the League collapsed with it. Here, again, the problem was not ignorance but cowardice. Member states recognised the dangers of appeasement but feared the consequences of confrontation. Without the will to bear costs, collective security was an empty phrase.

What is striking in retrospect is that the League's failures were not inevitable. The machinery for collective action existed. Reports were written, sanctions debated, diplomatic missions sent. But cooperation requires more than forums; it requires alignment of incentives and trust. In the 1930s, both were in short supply. Each state viewed international commitments through the lens of domestic political survival. Britain feared alienating voters already weary of war. France, haunted by demographic decline and political division, was obsessed with preserving alliances in Europe rather than projecting strength abroad. The United States, though economically dominant, retreated into isolationism. In such a climate, the League was less an actor than a stage on which national anxieties played out.

The League's impotence underscores a broader truth about international governance: institutions are only as strong as the political will that animates them. Crises reveal whether cooperation is a principle or a posture. The 1930s demonstrated that when material hardship and nationalist sentiment collide, the scaffolding of collective security collapses swiftly. Global order is not sustained by ideals alone but by credible commitments backed with resources and risk-taking. Without them, treaties become parchment barriers, swept aside by the first storm.

Yet the story is not merely one of institutional failure; it is also one of lessons learned. The collapse of the League informed the design of the post-1945 United Nations, with greater emphasis on enforcement mechanisms, financial institutions, and the participation of all major powers. But even these reforms could not erase the fundamental dilemma: global cooperation must coexist with the primacy of nation-states. The Depression revealed the depth of that tension, showing how fragile cooperative frameworks become when domestic legitimacy is at stake.

The question lingers, uncomfortably: are today's institutions any more resilient than the League was in 1931? Global crises—whether financial collapse, climate change, or pandemics—demand collective action, yet national governments remain pulled by domestic pressures and short-term horizons. The Great Depression's legacy is not only that cooperation failed, but that it exposed the structural challenge of international governance itself. Can nations act together when their electorates demand they act alone? The League's ghost continues to haunt us, a reminder that without unity in sacrifice, global order rests on the foundations of sand.

How Crisis Became Prelude to War

In 1932, a Berlin housewife queued for bread while outside the bakery a Nazi stormtrooper handed out pamphlets promising "work and honour" through national renewal. At the same time, across the globe in Japan, army officers were justifying the occupation of Manchuria as a means to secure rice, coal, and markets for a starving nation. These moments, though thousands of miles apart, reveal a common thread: economic collapse had breached the walls of domestic politics and was spilling outward into foreign aggression. The Depression was not just a story of shuttered factories and idle hands—it was the spark that lit the fuse of global conflict.

The paradox of the 1930s lies in how nations sought safety in ways that made the world more dangerous. Instead of cooperation, economic despair pushed states toward confrontation. Hunger was not only a social condition but also a geopolitical weapon. Factories without orders became rallying cries for protectionism; trade barriers became symbols of sovereignty; militarised expansion was reframed as economic strategy. What began as financial panic in New York and London became territorial seizures in Asia and Europe. The line between economic recovery and aggressive war blurred until, by decade's end, they were nearly indistinguishable.

Germany's trajectory is perhaps the starkest example. Weimar democracy had already been battered by inflation and humiliation after Versailles, but the Depression was the mortal blow. Unemployment surged to six million, bankruptcies mounted, and middle-class savings evaporated. Into this void stepped Hitler, whose appeal was as much economic as it was ideological. He promised bread for the hungry, jobs for the unemployed, and revenge against the powers that had reduced Germany to penury. The rearmament programme—presented as economic revival—was also preparation for war. Autobahns and armaments were two sides of the same coin: economic recovery fused with militarisation.

Japan's case demonstrates a different but complementary logic. Export collapse devastated silk and textile industries, leaving rural families destitute. Civilian governments faltered, paralysed by factionalism and bound by free-trade orthodoxy. Militarists filled the void with a compelling narrative: expansion into Manchuria would guarantee resources, markets, and national self-sufficiency. The invasion of 1931 was not random adventurism but a calculated response to economic desperation. By rebranding conquest as economic policy, Japan made external aggression seem not only legitimate but necessary. Here, as in Germany, the crisis turned inward insecurity into outward expansion.

Italy followed suit, though from a position of relative weakness. Mussolini had long promised to revive Italy's "proletarian nation" status by creating a new Roman Empire. The Depression intensified pressures—industrial contraction, rural unrest, and fragile finances—that made the conquest of Ethiopia in 1935 appear attractive. The campaign was justified as an economic safety valve, securing land and prestige that domestic reform could not deliver. In reality, it overextended Italy's economy, but it revealed how readily crises could be channelled into imperial dreams.

The democracies, too, were not immune to the pull of economic nationalism, though their strategies differed. Britain retreated into imperial preference, prioritising trade within its empire and tightening control over colonial resources. France, fearful of both economic collapse and German resurgence, doubled down on defensive alliances and protectionist policies. These were not acts of territorial aggression, but they nonetheless fractured the global economy and undermined the possibility of collective recovery. Each nation's retreat into economic self-preservation weakened the international system and emboldened those willing to gamble on war.

Underlying all these cases is a profound insight: economic fragility magnifies political choices, making radical solutions appear rational. When livelihoods collapse, the promise of stability—whether through authoritarian order or territorial conquest—becomes intoxicating. The Depression made it easy for leaders to frame aggression not as reckless but as rescue. Citizens, desperate for relief, proved willing to gamble on policies that would, in calmer times, have been unthinkable. The crisis did not invent authoritarianism or expansionism, but it legitimised them by cloaking them in the language of survival.

The consequences were cumulative. Each act of aggression—Japan in Manchuria, Italy in Ethiopia, Germany in reoccupying the Rhineland—went largely unpunished, further eroding the norms of peace. Economic collapse had not merely weakened nations internally; it had hollowed out the international order. The League of Nations, stripped of authority and credibility, became little more than a bystander. By the time Hitler annexed

Austria and demanded Czechoslovakia, aggression had become the default currency of international politics.

What makes this story resonate beyond its time is the uncomfortable recognition that economic collapse rarely stays confined within borders. It metastasises, reshaping geopolitics as surely as it reshapes domestic economies. The Depression reminds us that when societies believe they are fighting for survival, they can justify almost anything—repression, expansion, even war—as economic necessity. The bridges between unemployment and invasion, between hunger and conquest, are built not only by demagogues but by the logic of despair itself.

The unresolved question is whether the world has truly learned this lesson. Global crises still invite inward retreat and outward blame. Protectionism rises, alliances strain, and the rhetoric of national survival returns with familiar urgency. The 1930s show us not only how a crisis became prelude to war but also how quickly the ordinary politics of recovery can morph into extraordinary justifications for conflict. The warning lingers: when economies falter, the first casualty is not always prosperity—it may be peace.

Echoes for the Present

In the spring of 2008, television screens filled with images of bankers leaving Lehman Brothers with cardboard boxes in their arms. Outside, protesters waved placards warning that ordinary people—not financiers—would pay the price of the collapse. Around the world, markets tumbled, governments scrambled, and citizens looked on in disbelief. Eight decades separated this moment from the Wall Street Crash of 1929, yet the resonances were impossible to ignore: panic in the markets, paralysis in politics, and the creeping fear that the ground beneath society's feet was less stable than it seemed.

The parallel is not incidental. Every great economic rupture, whether in the 1930s or the twenty-first century, exposes a deeper truth: material prosperity is never just about numbers on a ledger. It is about trust, cohesion, and legitimacy. When those foundations crack, the consequences ripple outward, unsettling institutions, reshaping political landscapes, and, at times, destabilising international order itself. The Great Depression did not remain a "past" crisis—it provided a template, both cautionary and predictive, for the dilemmas modern societies continue to face.

Today's global economy operates at a pace and scale unimaginable to interwar policymakers. Supply chains stretch across continents; financial flows travel in milliseconds; pandemics can shutter economies overnight. Yet the vulnerabilities remain eerily familiar. Dependence on fragile trade networks echoes Britain's entanglement with free trade in the 1930s. The resurgence of populist politics recalls the authoritarian temptations that followed mass unemployment in Weimar Germany. And international organisations, whether the League of Nations then or the United Nations and WTO now, still struggle to enforce cooperation when national survival is at stake.

Consider how quickly fear spreads when markets seize. In the 1930s, a run on a single bank could trigger nationwide panic. In 2008, the collapse of Lehman Brothers cascaded into a global liquidity freeze. In 2020, the COVID-19 pandemic translated public health failures into economic paralysis. Each episode underscored a common reality: fear in the financial system is not abstract; it is lived in empty factories, shuttered shops, and anxious households. And when citizens see elites shielded from the worst effects while ordinary families bear the brunt, resentment takes on a political life of its own.

Here lies the enduring link between economic crisis and political extremism. Despair makes radical promises plausible. In the 1930s, fascists in Europe and militarists in Japan sold dreams of certainty and renewal to societies drowning in chaos. In the present, one hears echoes of that strategy in the rhetoric of populist leaders who frame outsiders—whether migrants, foreign competitors, or supranational institutions—as scapegoats for domestic decline. History does not repeat in identical form, but the emotional economy of fear and hope remains constant.

At the same time, crises can awaken reformist energies. The New Deal in the United States demonstrated how bold policy experimentation could restore faith in democracy rather than destroy it. Similarly, after 2008, governments introduced new regulations on banks, and after the pandemic, debates over social safety nets and supply-chain resilience gained fresh urgency. The direction a society takes in the aftermath of crisis depends less on the fact of economic pain than on the narratives through which that pain is interpreted. Does the moment demand solidarity and reform, or division and exclusion?

International cooperation, too, continues to falter under strain. In the 1930s, the League of Nations proved unable to check aggression or coordinate recovery. Today, climate summits falter, trade negotiations stall, and geopolitical rivalries obstruct collective action. The lesson of the Depression—that domestic crises cannot be contained when the world is interconnected—remains as relevant as ever. Yet institutions designed to provide solutions often resemble the League: ambitious on paper, hesitant in practice.

What the 1930s remind us is not that catastrophe is inevitable, but that complacency is dangerous. Democracies survived in some places, collapsed in others. Authoritarian regimes rose where fear overwhelmed hope, but they were not destined to succeed; they triumphed because too many citizens, disillusioned by economic failure, abandoned faith in fragile institutions. The past warns us that no society, however stable it seems, is immune from collapse when economic life falters and political will fractures.

The Depression's echoes reverberate most strongly in our own age of uncertainty. Climate disruption, technological upheaval, and widening inequality may prove as destabilising to the twenty-first century as financial collapse was to the twentieth. The warning from history is stark: economic fragility is never just about wealth. It is about power, legitimacy, and peace. Whether societies turn their crises into platforms for renewal or into pathways to conflict remains the unresolved question—a question as urgent now as it was when desperate citizens once looked to strongmen for salvation.

The 1930s are not a closed chapter. They are a mirror, one that reflects not only the dangers of economic collapse but also the enduring choices societies face when confronted by crisis. And as long as those choices remain ours to make, the echoes of that decade will continue to sound—not as distant history, but as a warning in the present tense.

About the Author

Felix Brandt writes with a historian's eye for pattern and a storyteller's instinct for human consequence. His work probes the fragile seams between economics and politics, where the collapse of trust can tip societies into chaos. Rooted in Europe yet looking outward, Brandt brings to life the voices of ordinary people caught in extraordinary upheavals, weaving them into a broader narrative of ideas, fears, and ambitions. His mission is to ask why democracies stumble, how extremism takes hold, and what lessons past crises hold for the present. Steeped in cultural memory and global history, his writing reminds readers that the fate of nations is often decided not in parliaments or markets, but in the daily struggle of citizens to endure, adapt, and believe in tomorrow.

www.ingramcontent.com/pod-product-compliance
Lightning Source LLC
Chambersburg PA
CBHW051354240926
51852CB00001B/19
9789390349401